YORK NOTES

A Choice of Poets

An anthology of poets from Wordsworth to the present day

Notes by Paul Pascoe

 Longman   York Press

YORK PRESS
322 Old Brompton Road, London SW5 9JH

Pearson Education Limited
Edinburgh Gate, Harlow,
Essex CM20 2JE, United Kingdom
Associated companies, branches and representatives throughout the world

First published 1997
Second impression 1999

ISBN 0–582–31335–X

Design by Vicki Pacey, Trojan Horse
Illustrated by Chris Brown
Phototypeset by Gem Graphics, Trenance, Mawgan Porth, Cornwall
Colour reproduction and film output by Spectrum Colour
Produced by Addison Wesley Longman China Limited, Hong Kong

Contents

PREFACE

York Notes are designed to give you a broader perspective on works of literature studied at GCSE and equivalent levels. We have carried out extensive research into the needs of the modern literature student prior to publishing this new edition. Our research showed that no existing series fully met students' requirements. Rather than present a single authoritative approach, we have provided alternative viewpoints, empowering students to reach their own interpretations of the text. York Notes provide a close examination of the work and include biographical and historical background, summaries, glossaries, analyses of characters, themes, structure and language, cultural connections and literary terms.

If you look at the Contents page you will see the structure for the series. However, there's no need to read from the beginning to the end as you would with a novel, play, poem or short story. Use the Notes in the way that suits you. Our aim is to help you with your understanding of the work, not to dictate how you should learn.

York Notes are written by English teachers and examiners, with an expert knowledge of the subject. They show you how to succeed in coursework and examination assignments, guiding you through the text and offering practical advice. Questions and comments will extend, test and reinforce your knowledge. Attractive colour design and illustrations improve clarity and understanding, making these Notes easy to use and handy for quick reference.

York Notes are ideal for:
- Essay writing
- Exam preparation
- Class discussion

The author of these Notes is Paul Pascoe, who has been a Chief and Principal Examiner in English since 1978. Author of a number of textbooks for Secondary pupils, he was until recently head of English at Formby High Comprehensive School.

The text used in these Notes is from *A Choice of Poets*, edited and chosen by R. P. Hewett (Nelson, 1968; this edition 1989).

Health Warning: **This study guide will enhance your understanding, but should not replace the reading of the original text and/or study in class.**

Part one

Introduction

How to study a poem

You have bought this book because you wanted to study poetry on your own. This may supplement work done in class.

- Look at the poem. How are the lines organised? Are they in groups? Are any lines repeated? Are any of the lines shorter or longer than the others? Try to think of reasons why the poet set out the lines in this way.
- Do lots of the lines end with a comma or a full stop – or does the sense carry over on to another line? What is the effect of stopping at the end of each line?
- Read the poem out aloud (or aloud in your head). Does the poem rhyme? If so, what words rhyme? Is this important ? Do some lines almost rhyme? Do some lines have rhyming words inside the line? If there is no rhyme, think about why the poet stops each line where he/she does.
- Read the poem aloud again. Think about the rhythm. Listen for the stressed words. Does the pattern of stressed and unstressed syllables create any kind of mood? Does it match the mood or subject-matter of the poem? Have some words been chosen for their sound?
- What is the poem about? Do not make up your mind too soon. Your first thoughts need to be reassessed when you reach the end. Remember that the subject-matter and the theme or idea of the poem may not be the same.
- Do any words make you stop and think? Are there interesting or unusual combinations of words? (Check the meaning of any words which puzzle you – they may have a meaning you are not familiar with.)

- Do a lot of the words seem to belong to one kind? Verbs, for example. Or are there a lot of words with similar meanings? Why?

Studying on your own requires self-discipline and a carefully thought-out work plan in order to be effective. Good luck.

HISTORICAL & SOCIAL CONTEXT

The poems in this selection cover a period of about two hundred years from the late eighteenth century to the present day. There have obviously been huge changes in our world in that time. Blake, Wordsworth and Keats saw the beginnings of the Industrial Revolution, which was to change the face of Britain. The period also witnessed the French Revolution and the demand for freedom from oppression became a rallying call throughout Europe. The desire for liberty was fuelled by the dreadful poverty endured by the poor, especially in the cities.

At the same time as there were demands for social change, artists were stressing the importance of the individual imagination, as what is known as the Romantic Movement swept Europe.

The social pressures are most evident in the poetry of Blake. His work is shot through with powerful images drawn from the emerging industries and he felt a burning anger at the appalling suffering he saw about him. The pain of living informs the poetry of Wordsworth and Keats, too, but usually in a more general way as in the sad song of 'The Solitary Reaper'. However, both these poets pursued the ideals of Romanticism and cherished the world of the imagination above all else.

By the second half of the nineteenth century the cities were still grim places but there was considerable belief in progress. Social reform and improvements in water supplies and sanitation did much to alleviate living conditions. However, the enormous developments in scientific knowledge led to other problems. The certainties of Biblical truth were called into question, especially after the publication of Darwin's treatise, *On the Origin of Species* in 1859. Many thinking people were shaken by doubt, not only concerning Christian faith but about the direction the world was taking. Even Hopkins, whose belief in God was strong, spent the last years of his life in despair.

Eliot pointed out the meaningless nature of modern life.

By the first quarter of the twentieth century the world had become recognisably modern. The effects of mass production, big business, the beginnings of mass communications were all working their way into people's lives and, of course, between 1914 and 1918 the horrors of technological warfare were unleashed in Europe for the first time. T.S. Eliot, essentially a poet of urban life, reacted to these changes by identifying a sense of meaningless triviality and emptiness at the core of society. The problems that Eliot found still tax people today.

One of the most important developments over the last century has been the rise of psychology and an increasing fascination with what makes us tick. In many ways, the poets in this selection both anticipate and reflect our increasing interest in the workings of the mind. A high proportion of the poems may be considered, on a superficial reading, as broadly pastoral, being concerned with some aspect of country life. Closer inspection will reveal that the poetry presents landscapes of the mind; the centre of interest in so many of these poems is not trees, rivers or mountains, but the poet's state of mind and the private world of his imagination. In that sense, the poets are not tied to particular time or place and all may be considered modern.

Industrial Revolution begins, and people start to move from the countryside to the cities	1750	
	1757	Birth of William Blake
Romantic movement begins	1770	Birth of William Wordsworth
The American Revolution	1775-83	
	1788	Birth of Lord Byron
French Revolution	1789-95	1795 Birth of John Keats
Napoleonic Wars	1795-	
Peninsular Wars	1801	
	1808-14	Birth of Alfred, Lord Tennyson
	1809	Death of John Keats
	1821	Death of Lord Byron
First railway passenger trains	1824	
	1825	Death of William Blake
Britain abolishes slavery	1827	
Queen Victoria accedes to the throne	1833	
Invention of photography	1837	Birth of Thomas Hardy
	1840	Birth of Gerard Manley Hopkins
	1844	
Charles Darwin publishes: *On the Origin of Species*	1850	Death of William Wordsworth
First bicycle	1859	
First typewriters	1865	
	1873	
	1874	Birth of Robert Frost
First telephone in use	1877	
	1878	Birth of Edward Thomas
First petrol-driven car		Birth of D.H. Lawrence

	1888	Birth of T.S. Eliot
	1889	Death of Gerard Manley Hopkins
	1892	Death of Alfred, Lord Tennyson
	1893	
First film shows	**1895**	Birth of Wilfred Owen
		Birth of Robert Graves
Sigmund Freud's *The Interpretation of Dreams* heralds the development of psycho-analysis	**1900**	
	1901	
Death of Queen Victoria	**1907**	
First aeroplane	**1913**	Birth of W.H. Auden
	1914-18	Birth of R.S. Thomas
First World War	**1917**	
The Russian Revolution	**1918**	Death of Edward Thomas
Women over 30 get the vote	**1920s**	Death of Wilfred Owen
The Jazz Age	**1922**	
First regular radio broadcasts	**1926**	
General Strike	**1930**	
	1930s	Death of D.H. Lawrence
The Great Depression	**1930s-45**	
Nazi persecution of the Jews	**1939-45**	
The Second World War	**1945**	
Beginning of the Cold War	**1946**	
First regular TV broadcasts in Britain	**1963**	
	1965	Death of Robert Frost
	1973	Death of T.S. Eliot
	1985	Death of W.H. Auden
		Death of Robert Graves

PART TWO

SUMMARIES

WILLIAM WORDSWORTH (1770–1850)

BACKGROUND

Wordsworth is closely associated with the Lake District, where he was born and where he spent a substantial part of his life, but his background was that of a well-educated, widely travelled gentleman.

He was born, the son of a lawyer, at Cockermouth in Cumberland. He was educated at Hawkshead Grammar School and St John's College, Cambridge, obtaining his BA degree in 1791.

Involvement with France

In 1790 he went on a walking tour which took him through France to Italy. The journey over the Alps was still a relatively rare, but increasingly popular, experience for those wanting to witness nature at her most 'sublime'. He returned to France in 1791 where he remained for a year. At that time, he had passionate belief in the French Revolution and its ideals of freedom and equality. He also had an affair with Annette Vallon by whom he had a daughter. These formative years are recorded in his long autobiographical poem, *The Prelude*. His enthusiasm for the French Revolution was soon dispelled by the Reign of Terror and England's declaration of war against France. However, his greatest poetry was still to speak for the spirit of freedom as represented in the imagination, if not in day-to-day social and political affairs.

Wordsworth was at first enthusiastic about the ideals of the French Revolution.

In 1795 he inherited sufficient money to become a full-time poet and the next twenty years saw his most productive period. He was much influenced by his friend, the poet and critic, Samuel Taylor Coleridge, and together, in 1798, they produced *Lyrical Ballads* which is regarded as a landmark in English poetry.

The Lake District

In 1799, with his sister, Dorothy, he settled in Dove Cottage, Grasmere.

In 1802 Wordsworth married Mary Hutchinson, with whom he had attended the infants' school in Penrith.

His popularity and public standing steadily increased and he formed friendships with some of the most prominent figures of the day.

In 1813 he moved to Rydal Mount, Ambleside, where he remained for the rest of his life. By now, he was an increasingly prosperous pillar of the establishment. He remained a prodigious walker and traveller in Britain and on the Continent. Many of these journeys are recorded in his later poetry, which though accomplished, tends to be gently descriptive or reflective and lacking the excitement of his earlier work.

In 1842 he was given a civil pension of £300 a year and he became Poet Laureate the following year.

THE SOLITARY REAPER

This haunting poem has no 'plot' or any obvious moral. It records a chance encounter with a girl reaping a field in some unspecified part of the Scottish Highlands.

The poet reflects upon the song that seems to swell to fill the valley. He likens it to the song of the nightingale and the call of the cuckoo, and wonders what the mysterious words may mean. They may tell of legendary events or more homely matters but they lead the poet to think of sad things. But of whatever the girl sang, the image of her bent over her work and the sound of her voice lingered in the poet's mind long after the sounds had died away.

COMMENT   The poem does not describe the girl as such, but
captures how the memory of her singing took a hold on
the poet's imagination.

The girl is alone and of humble origin. Both these
characteristics appear time and time again in
Wordsworth's poetry. The notion of solitariness was
very common in literature of the time throughout
Europe, as writers concentrated on the inner world of
personal feeling. Wordsworth also believed that people
of humble origin, especially country-dwellers, were
closer to the source of natural human feeling than the
wealthier and more sophisticated (see also 'The World
is Too Much With Us' below).

The song seems to   The reaper's song is 'melancholy' and 'plaintive' and
reach beyond the   may tell of 'sorrow, loss or pain' but it is also 'thrilling'.
valley.   The blend of joy and sorrow and a feeling for the
bitter-sweet qualities of life were shared by many artists
of the day. Keats explores some very similar ideas in
'Ode to a Nightingale'.

Curiously, although the poem reads like a personal
reminiscence, Wordsworth noted that it was inspired by
a line in an account of a tour to Scotland written by a
friend, Thomas Wilkinson. The last line of the poem is
virtually a quotation from his friend's work. However,
in her *Recollections*, Dorothy Wordsworth recalled
seeing the reapers in the fields at harvest-time and
recorded that it was 'not uncommon in the more lonely
parts of the Highlands to see a single person so
employed'. This background information is interesting
because it indicates how a merest hint can sometimes
fire a poet's imagination.

from
THE PRELUDE (1)

This famous extract from Book I (Childhood and
School-time) of the long autobiographical poem tells of

the impression left on the poet by a childhood prank which led him into one of his most vivid and disturbing encounters with nature.

The 'grim shape' is more frightening than a 'craggy steep'.

The poet finds a small boat tethered by the lakeside and decides to take it for an evening expedition. Feeling guilty because he has taken it without permission, he makes his way across the lake, leaving silvery circles shimmering in the moonlight as his oars break the water. As he rows he sets his sights on a 'craggy ridge' so as to keep a straight course. At first he is aware only of the vastness of the night sky, the silence of the lake and his tiny craft. Gradually, however, a huge mountain peak looms into view and seems to grow threateningly, blotting out the sky, as though it were alive and following the young boy. Frightened by the sight, the poet turns about, returns to the shore, leaving the boat in its mooring place, and heads for home in 'serious mood'. As the days pass, his mind is disturbed by the memory of his experience. The normal boyhood pleasure in the countryside and its sights gives way to the presence in his mind of huge, dark, living shapes that seem to have their own forms of existence.

from
THE PRELUDE (2)

Note his companions are not described in detail.

In this second extract, the poet is physically in the company of other children, but once again the forces of nature lead him into a very private and solitary experience. The poet and his companions were skating excitedly, wholly oblivious of approaching darkness and had no thoughts of returning home. They played games chasing each other and imitating the sounds of the hunt. Their voices echoed around the surrounding frozen hills.

Far off, the distant hills, the stars and the fading sunset seemed to offer a strangely sad contrast to the hubbub on the ice.

The poet was given to breaking away from the other skaters to find a quiet corner for himself or to chasing the reflection of a star in the ice. Frequently, as the skaters were swept along by the winds at their backs, the poet spun round and, stopping short, experienced the sensation of the cliffs spinning past him as though the world itself were in visible movement.

Compare with the ending of Keats's 'Ode to a Nightingale'.

Gradually, as the light gave out, the scene became still and peaceful, as if it were a dream.

COMMENT   Both these extracts are drawn from Wordsworth's long autobiographical poem. The subtitle *Growth of a Poet's Mind* is important because, although the poem naturally contains much factual detail, it is really concerned with the development of the imagination. In this respect childhood and contact with nature were vital for Wordsworth.

Compare the ways in which the young Wordsworth felt that nature was his teacher.

Both extracts begin with a relatively commonplace event which develops into something profound and unforgettable. A similar pattern is to be found in 'Nutting'. In the boating incident the first twenty lines evoke the excitement of a boyish escapade but with the sudden appearance of the huge black peak, the experience takes a different and frightening turn. Similarly, the first eighteen lines of the skating episode paint an energetic picture of frantic pleasure but from then on the poet is overawed by the vision of the surrounding vastness.

Notice that the poet is effectively alone in both incidents – the other skaters are only vaguely represented.

In both these incidents the poet is demonstrating the power of natural objects to impress themselves on one's emotional and imaginative life. In the boating incident, the boy's guilt at stealing the boat is shaped and

y

amplified by his sense of terror at the looming mountain. In the second extract, he undergoes a trance-like experience (partly induced by his dizziness) in which he forgets his companions and comes to feel in tune with the profound forces of nature.

Notice how Wordsworth suggests how nature can inhabit the imagination by referring to natural features as 'shapes', 'spectacle', 'images', and 'forms' rather than describing them in detail.

GLOSSARY   **bark** boat
                  chiming musical sound made by hounds

THE WORLD IS TOO MUCH WITH US

Think about ways   In the first section, the poet laments the distractions
other poets would and concerns of daily life. Superficially, they lead to
share   prosperity, but we have sacrificed our ability to feel any
Wordsworth's   unity with nature.
concern.
                     The poet imagines himself looking out to sea and
                     stands in awe of the huge forces that are gathering, but
                     modern society is untouched by such feelings.

                     In the second part, the poet expresses his personal anger
                     and frustration. It would be better to be a pagan. At
                     least, his imagination would be alive with visions of the
                     ancient gods of the sea.

C OMMENT   This sonnet (see Literary Terms) deals with what has
                    become a particularly modern theme; the way that the
                    pressures and habits of everyday living tend to
                    dehumanise us.

                    The poem is not merely a protest about our rush to
                    acquire material prosperity but is an attack on the
                    failure to experience life and nature with the full force
                    of the imagination.

                    The classical references are included to suggest that

however primitive we may consider pagan societies to be, they felt a oneness with their environment which they peopled with living gods.

GLOSSARY   **suckled** nursed
            creed religious belief
            wreathed entwined with seaweed

TO A SKYLARK

In the first stanza the poet asks whether the skylark hovering invisibly high in the sky shows contempt for the earth with all its troubles.

Alternatively, he wonders whether the skylark can belong to two realms, the sky and the earth, because it can both sing high in the air and drop directly to its nest on the ground.

As in 'The Solitary Reaper' the poet finds a wider meaning to the song.

In the second stanza, he answers his questions by praising the skylark for its ability to pour out its divine song from on high and also for teaching us that it is possible to aspire to higher things and at the same time be true to our natural selves.

COMMENT   The skylark has proved an attractive subject for poets, most famously Shelley, because its song seems to fill the air while the bird itself hovers invisibly in the summer sky.

GLOSSARY   **kindred** related

NUTTING

The poem begins with very ordinary matters.

The poem falls into four sections. The first, lines 1–14, describes setting out on the search for hazelnuts, with the familiar insistence by the woman who was looking after him that he should wear his oldest clothes.

Lines 14–25 give an account of the search, how he scrambled through brambles and overgrown woods until the poet found a totally untouched hazel grove.

Lines 25–43, the centre of the poem, comprise an interlude, in which the poet explains how he lay beneath the trees and breathed in the gentleness of the scene.

Compare the poet's guilt here with what he felt when he stole the boat. The last section recalls how he harvested the nuts by pulling at the branches, often breaking them in the process. However, although he was overjoyed at being able to gather such a rich crop, at the same time he felt guilty that he had harmed nature. The poet concludes that there was a spirit in nature that taught him to be gentle.

COMMENT   Like the extracts from *The Prelude* this is a recollection of childhood. Wordsworth recalled: 'Like most of my school fellows I was an impassioned nutter'.

Once again, an ordinary boyhood activity develops into an encounter with the moral force of nature. As in the boating incident, the young boy is left feeling chastened but with an appreciation of nature's gentleness rather than its terror.

GLOSSARY   **weeds** old clothes

husbanded saved

Dame Ann Tyson, with whom the poet stayed when he was at grammar school

sate an old form of 'sat'

temper mood

dearest Maiden the poem was originally addressed to Lucy

COMPOSED UPON WESTMINSTER BRIDGE

The first part of this famous sonnet (see Literary Terms) presents a vision of London in early morning. The poet shows the scene from a distance, so that the

The poet uses a succession of words to suggest silence and immobility. features of the urban environment seems transformed and merge with the sky and the surrounding countryside.

In the second part the poet is moved to feel that this vision of London in all its serenity is the equal of any of his experiences in the natural world.

COMMENT Wordsworth did not like cities as 'The World is Too Much With Us' suggests, but in this sonnet, London is described as if it were part of a grand natural landscape.

The poem is impressionistic and there is none of the close-up detail that is found in Blake's 'London'.

LUCY POEMS

Poem I The poet, travelling abroad, thinks back to Lucy, sitting beside the fire spinning, and realises he loves her.

Poem II Lucy was an unknown girl who is now dead.

Poem III Lucy, while she lived, was like an ethereal being; now that she is dead she has become as one with nature.

COMMENT These poems are admired for the powerful emotional force Wordsworth was able to achieve with the sparest language.

There is no evidence that Lucy ever existed, though it seems likely that she may be modelled, in part at least, on the poet's image of his sister. Whoever she may have been, she acts as a focus for Wordsworth's feelings of longing, joy and sense of loss.

Poem I was, in fact, the last of this group to be composed. It was written in Germany where Wordsworth and his sister became desperately homesick. Lucy becomes the embodiment of England and the focus of his longing.

In Poem II Lucy is depicted as a kind of nymph, a half-glimpsed creature of nature, of rare beauty.

The last two lines gain their power from their absolute simplicity. They state the sense of loss without any unnecessary explanation.

Poem III expresses desolation at the death of Lucy whose innocent spirit seemed beyond the clutches of mortality and, at the same time, a kind of consolation that she is now securely enshrined in nature.

THEMES, LANGUAGE & STYLE

Wordsworth is most popularly known as a nature poet closely associated with the English Lake District. There is no doubt that like most of the Romantic artists throughout Europe, Wordsworth felt a close affinity with nature which is rarely absent from his poetry.

Like many of his contempories, Wordsworth discovered a simplicity and purity in the natural environment which contrasted with the constrictions and artificiality of urban life. He felt that the rural environment and its people offered closer contact with essential, uncorrupted values and eternal truths.

Compare Wordsworth's attitudes to nature with those of Frost and Thomas.

Wordsworth also seems to claim that nature is a teacher offering moral guidance, especially to the child (see *The Prelude* I and 'Nutting'). It has often been suggested that Wordsworth was a *pantheist*, that is, that he believed that there was a divine spirit throughout creation.

However, a close reading of his poetry reveals that Wordsworth was less concerned with nature as such, as with the workings of his own imagination. Significantly, *The Prelude* is subtitled *Growth of a Poet's Mind* and a constant feature of his poetry is that he does not describe the landscape directly but refers to the 'shapes', 'images', 'forms', 'spectacles', etc. which are implanted in his mind and recreated in his *memory*.

Even his famous daffodils flashed upon 'the inward eye'. The true power of nature lay in his own imagination.

Today we are familiar, through film and television, with the workings of psychology and the dramas that are played out in our own minds. Wordsworth was one of the first writers to explore the landscape of the private imagination.

Wordsworth also believed that it was necessary to write in the 'real language of men' and attacked the artificiality of eighteenth-century poetry with its specialised language and so-called 'poetic diction'. It is doubtful whether phrases such as 'the earth's diurnal course' or 'elfin pinnace' could be classed as common language but, particular expressions aside, Wordsworth was at times able to convey something of a sense of an easy flow of thought, as in the opening of 'Nutting'.

A *Identify the poems from which these words are taken.*

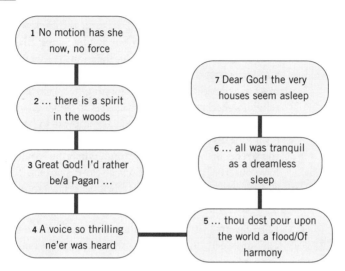

1 No motion has she now, no force

2 ... there is a spirit in the woods

3 Great God! I'd rather be/a Pagan ...

4 A voice so thrilling ne'er was heard

7 Dear God! the very houses seem asleep

6 ... all was tranquil as a dreamless sleep

5 ... thou dost pour upon the world a flood/Of harmony

Check your answers on page 96.

B *Consider these issues.*

a The influence of nature on the young Wordsworth.

b The importance of the imagination to Wordsworth.

c People in Wordsworth's poetry are almost always solitary, whether they are characters like the Reaper, or the poet himself. Even the other children in the skating episode are just a vague impression.

d Wordsworth is more concerned with showing how nature can affect our imagination and live in our memory than with mere description.

e Why the author claimed that poetry was 'recollection in tranquillity'.

WILLIAM BLAKE (1757–1827)

BACKGROUND

Like Keats, Blake was a Londoner. His father was a hosier and William, the third of seven children, was born over the family shop in Soho. The young Blake did not go to school but was an incessant reader and, as a result, accumulated a wide but unconventional body of knowledge. His parents, belonging to a 'dissenting' religious sect, were staunch believers in social justice and opponents of corruption. Blake appears to have been a fiercely independent child, given to wandering the streets of London and beyond, where he would have observed social conditions at close quarters. These early influences appear to have been the springboard for his life's work.

Blake's upbringing gave him first-hand experience of poverty and suffering as well as developed his imagination.

His powerful visual imagination was recognised early and after attending drawing school he was apprenticed as an engraver in 1772 and became a student at the Royal Academy in 1778.

In 1782 he married Catherine Boucher, the daughter of a market-gardener and, in the next forty-five years till Blake's death, they appear to have been apart for only two or three weeks.

His first volume of poetry, *Poetical Sketches* was published in 1783.

His *Songs of Innocence* were published in 1789, using his own system of 'Illuminated Printing'. The *Songs of Experience* followed in 1794.

These early works already display many elements of the complex mystical vision he was to develop in such works as *The Book of Urizen* (1794), *The Song of Los* (1795*)*, *The Book of Ahania* (1795), *The Book of Los* (1795), *The Four Zoas* (1797–1804) and *Jerusalem* (1804–20).

Blake was passionately devoted to freedom and social justice and was an enthusiastic supporter of the French Revolution. He detested institutions and all forms of oppression and was even charged with high treason for cursing the king.

His writing was not popular, however, and his later years were spent in poverty and obscurity, although his work as an engraver attracted the admiration of a circle of young artists.

Much of Blake's writing is extremely obscure but the power of his language, his ability to make words sing and his belief in justice and the integrity of all things have continued to appeal, especially to those with a rebellious turn of mind.

ON ANOTHER'S SORROW

The poet draws a parallel between human feeling for another person's pain and God's feeling for His creation.

Blake uses a question and answer technique for effect.

The poet asks whether a father and a mother can fail to respond to the needs of the child in their care. Answer comes back that they cannot, they must not. Likewise, can God fail to care for the vulnerable within his creation? The answer must be the same.

Consequently, not only the infant, but all of us may rely on God's comfort.

COMMENT   Like *Auguries of Innocence* this poem concerns itself with the correspondence between small aspects of life and the universal and eternal concerns of the divine. The idea of the unity of creation, in this case reflected in the desire for consolation and comfort, is a powerful thread in Blake's poetry.

THE DIVINE IMAGE and A DIVINE IMAGE

These poems provide violently contrasting views of the image of God as seen in man. 'The Divine Image' is organised as an argument which comprises a series of statements leading to a conclusion. The basic argument is roughly:

Men pray to the 'virtues of delight' in gratitude (stanza 1) because these virtues together compose God, but these virtues together also compose man (stanza 2), because each of these virtues has a distinct human form (stanza 3). Therefore when men pray to the virtues they are in fact praying to the divine which is represented in man (stanza 4). Consequently, whatever our religion we should worship the human form because God is found in it (stanza 5).

The references to forging and the furnace suggest the violence of an iron-foundry.

By contrast, 'A Divine Image' picks up stanza 3 of 'The Divine Image' with the proposition that just as mercy, pity, peace and love are represented in the human form so are the corresponding qualities, cruelty, jealousy, terror and secrecy. But if the human form is divine, then the second, perverted set of qualities is an aspect of that divinity.

COMMENT

The starting point for both these poems is the belief that man was created in the image of God; if that is so, in what ways is the reverse true?

Blake was a deeply religious man but he detested institutionalised churches and narrow doctrine (see 'The Garden of Love'). Consequently, in 'The Divine Image' he argues that God's benevolence is universal and not restricted to Christianity.

The constant repetition of the words 'Mercy, Pity, Peace and Love' emphasises how much these are the essential qualities of God in man.

Y

'A Divine Image' represents a perversion of the values of the first poem, but for Blake the darker side of human nature was also a facet of creation.

The distinction between the definite and indirect articles ('the' and 'a') in the titles of the poems perhaps suggests that the latter is in some way contained within the former.

THE TYGER

Spelt in the anthology as 'The Tiger', this famous poem is far easier to respond to than it is to explain.

A powerful contrast between light and darkness runs through the poem.

Broadly speaking, the poem establishes a sense of awe and wonder at the image (see Literary Terms) of a fierce but brilliant creature and the fearsome power it embodies. The poem proceeds by means of a succession of images and unanswerable questions that explore the origin and nature of the terrible but mysterious creature. Who *could* have created such a creature in all its aspects and what frightening powers were needed to do so? Was it the same as created the gentle lamb? Who would *dare* form such a creature?

COMMENT

The tiger is associated in Blake's writings with wrath and fear. Biblical references and contemporary writings on natural history confirmed the image of lions and tigers being particularly ferocious and ravenous beasts. Blake could have seen tigers in captivity; two were kept at the Tower of London.

Whatever the poem may 'mean', its undeniable power lies in the sense that the tiger is a stupendous creation, whose ferocity seems to call in doubt all the qualities represented in 'The Divine Image' and symbolised (see Literary Terms) here by the lamb.

The 'fearful symmetry' may signify the terrible conflict between peace and destructiveness, symbolised by the

tiger and which exists in creation and even in the
human mind; on a simpler level it may even bring to
mind a tiger's markings.

Blake's illustrations of the 'tyger' sometimes show
a ferocious creature, at other times depict
something resembling a domestic cat, apparently
smiling.

Compare the various possible meanings of 'garden' in 'The Garden of Love'.

Individual phrases are memorable for their simplicity
but suggest complex meanings. 'Burning bright' may
suggest the tiger's eyes glowing in the dark (one
account that Blake studied, referred to the 'tyger cat ...
with its eyes emitting flashes like lightning'), but
'burning' also suggests passion while 'bright' may be
associated with radiance and glory.

The furnace and the anvil relate to the process of
forging (See also 'A Divine Image' and 'London') which
is associated with intense violence. Here Blake is asking
what supreme creative force had the power to bring the
tiger into being. The process of producing the copper
plates which Blake used for his engravings used
considerable force and energy.

GLOSSARY   **symmetry** balance of shape and form

THE CLOD AND THE PEBBLE

The poem presents us with two contrasting visions of
love. The clod is unselfish and sees love as giving joy to
others. The pebble, on the other hand, defines love in
terms of the pleasure it can gain for itself, at another's
expense.

COMMENT   The clod, which is soft and pliable, sings a song of
innocence, while the hard and unyielding pebble sings a
song of experience.

HOLY THURSDAY

The poet looks on at the annual service of thanksgiving in St Paul's Cathedral attended by charity school children dressed in their best clothes.

The word 'appall'
is also powerfully
used in 'London'.

He is led to question why the children of such a rich country should be reduced to poverty at all. As they sing at the service, he hears no sound of joy. Why is it, he asks, that these children are cast into the wilderness when a country with such a climate as ours should provide for all?

COMMENT

In the simplest reading, the poem represents direct moral outrage that in a wealthy country, so many children should be starving.

However, the fact that the image at the core of the poem is a 'celebration' in St Paul's Cathedral attended by the neatly dressed charity school children of London also raises issues of hypocrisy and the true motives of those who administer charity.

Blake's passionate belief in social justice is revealed in his readiness to criticise an event which most people would regard as a happy occasion.

THE GARDEN OF LOVE

The garden, a symbol (see Literary Terms) of innocence and freedom, possibly sexual freedom, has been despoiled by the construction of a chapel.

The chapel does not enlighten, it only censors.

Note how sinister
the priests seem.

The speaker attempts to return to the garden but finds it has become a graveyard in which all the flowers, images of pleasure and freedom, have been choked by the dark agents of the Church.

COMMENT   The poem is an outspoken attack on the Church. It is depicted here as a despoiler which chokes off individual faith.

The image of the garden has multiple associations in literature. It is a place of beauty and tranquillity where children may play. It may also be a reminder of the Garden of Eden and lost innocence.

INFANT SORROW

Blake takes a very fierce and uncomfortable view of infancy. Birth is a struggle for parents and child alike. The child 'leaps' into the world protesting, as though ready to do battle with its dangers. At the same time, it settles for biding its time quietly on the mother's breast.

COMMENT   This concentrated poem presents a contrasting, possibly unusual, view of birth. On the one hand, there is the traditional picture of an infant's helplessness and dependency; on the other, Blake sees the child as entering the world already prepared for battle in a hostile environment.

LONDON   The horrors of life for the poor in Blake's 'London' are captured in a series of vivid images (see Literary Terms). The poet is to be imagined as a helpless observer touring the streets of the city.

The repetition of 'every' hammers home the universality of the suffering among the ordinary people.

The dreadful universality of the desolation is stressed in the first two stanzas. The cause of such dreadful suffering appears to be the man-made laws, codes and customs which effectively oppress and imprison these people.

The last two stanzas depict the corruption of values by the use of images which combine contrasting notions of good and evil, life and death.

COMMENT

In this poem Blake is most obviously outspoken against social injustice. The poem takes much of its force from the circumstances under which it was composed.

It was written in 1792 when popular support for the French Revolution was at its height. The spring had been unseasonably hot with temperatures reaching 82°F in March and English and German troops were posted around London to guard against public unrest.

The Church as so often is singled for particular criticism by Blake and is specifically linked with childhood suffering (See also 'Holy Thursday').

Troops were sent on manoeuvre in readiness to defend the Crown and the government against insurrection. Many suffered badly.

It is recorded that there were 50,000 prostitutes in London at the time.

GLOSSARY   **manacles** handcuffs

NEVER SEEK TO TELL THY LOVE

There is something about the deepest nature of love that one should not attempt to express. The central mystery cannot and should not be put into words.

The speaker, however, felt a need to do so and as a

result lost his love who was taken by the mysterious 'traveller'.

COMMENT   This poem gains its power from the way that it suggests meaning rather than states it.

The 'traveller' could be the figure of Death, a notion which matches the chilling mood of the conclusion, but much the poem's power lies in the way that Blake has *not* been explicit.

from

AUGURIES OF INNOCENCE

The reference to 'ruin of the State' reminds us of Blake's revolutionary views.

The extract comprises an introductory statement of the poet's theme, that the wonder and vastness of Eternity is contained in even the smallest things, followed by a long series of couplets warning that an offence against the seemingly insignificant or innocent (from the robin, the dove, the horse to the fly, the moth or the butterfly) is, in fact, an offence against the Eternal Order. The reverse is also true; to allow the wolf its freedom or the deer to live unharmed elevates humankind.

COMMENT   The poem expresses outrage at the thoughtless cruelty with which man treats fellow creatures.

More importantly, perhaps, the poet is stressing the physical, mental and spiritual unity of existence.

The simple couplet form with its proverbial overtones is closely related to popular verse that could be bought from stalls on the streets of London.

GLOSSARY   **augury** an omen or prophecy
cherubim a kind of angel

y

A POISON TREE

In four short stanzas this poem declares how a natural, if undesirable emotion, anger, can lead through dishonesty and deceit to destructive hate and hypocrisy.

The speaker suggests that anger is an honest emotion which once openly shared with a friend did not last.

When he concealed his anger from an enemy, it began to grow (like a sapling tree).

He fostered his feelings in private, but behaved falsely and deceitfully to his enemy.

The 'apple bright' reminds us of the temptation of Adam and Eve.

Eventually, it was the enemy who grew jealous and showed his spite first, feelings which led him to seek revenge.

The speaker, seeing his foe's moral collapse, is triumphant.

COMMENT

The poem is written as a warning to show how the repression of anger can lead to hatred; the triumph expressed at the end is ironic (see Literary Terms).

The poet emerges apparently unblemished but, in fact, corrupted by his own dishonesty.

GLOSSARY   **the pole** the tree

THEMES, LANGUAGE & STYLE

Blake's interests and views were extremely complex but two interwoven concerns run through all his work: social justice and understanding of the divine order of things.

From personal observation and conviction, he was a passionate defender of the rights of the individual and attacked the institutions of power which he felt

y

enslaved the populace. 'Holy Thursday' and 'London',
for instance, express anger and outrage at the very
existence of poverty and oppression. In the wake of the
American Declaration of Independence and the French
Revolution, such thoughts were considered dangerous
in established quarters.

Blake was equally critical of rationalist thought, which
was giving rise to the development of science and the
Industrial Revolution. He was concerned that people
would become no more than cogs in a vast, impersonal,
materialist machine.

*Consider how
Blake's poetry
almost always
reveals contrasting
aspects of life and
existence.*

Underpinning these particular concerns was a deep
religious conviction which he inherited from his
parents. But Blake did not belong to any orthodox
church; he disliked church institutions as much as any
other (see 'The Garden of Love'). Instead, he evolved
his own mystical beliefs, which, though very
complicated, stress at heart the wholeness of a complex
creation. (The extract from *Auguries of Innocence* and
'The Tyger' provide something of the flavour of Blake's
vision.)

Blake's universe was one of extremes: of love and
violence, of good and evil and of innocence and
experience – broadly, the innocence associated with the
Garden of Eden before Man sinned, and the experience
represented by the world since. However, the
distinctions are never clear, as all these qualities are
simultaneously present in creation. Blake believed that
to achieve true humanity and justice, we should be open
to all possibilities and appreciate how the physical and
spiritual reflect one another.

Blake's views may be difficult to grasp but his poetry
has a music all of its own. Compared with his
contemporary, Wordsworth, Blake employs few obscure
words to bother the modern reader and there is a

Y

directness and clarity in his phrasing, as in the opening of 'The Tyger', which remains in the memory, whatever the words ultimately mean.

The ingredients of Blake's poems are often extremely simple. He makes frequent use of simple rhetorical devices such as repetition, question and exclamation. He also makes full use of clear rhymes (see Literary Terms) which tend to throw weight on to key words, most vividly perhaps in 'London', in which each line builds towards its conclusion.

A *Identify the poems from which these words are taken.*

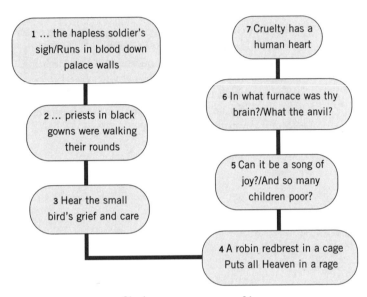

1 ... the hapless soldier's sigh/Runs in blood down palace walls

2 ... priests in black gowns were walking their rounds

3 Hear the small bird's grief and care

7 Cruelty has a human heart

6 In what furnace was thy brain?/What the anvil?

5 Can it be a song of joy?/And so many children poor?

4 A robin redbrest in a cage Puts all Heaven in a rage

Check your answers on page 96.

B *Consider these issues.*

a How Blake conv vs his belief that there is both beauty and violence in God's creation.

b What Blake means by Innocence and Experience.

c How Blake reveals his anger at suffering and injustice.

d The part that repetition plays in Blake's poetry. He may repeat words, phrases or sentence patterns.

e The evidence that Blake drew on his observations of people and industry of the world about him.

JOHN KEATS (1795–1821)

BACKGROUND

John Keats was one of the most richly talented of all English poets, a fact made all the more remarkable by the difficulties of his short life. His poetry speaks of romantic worlds and far off places but he was a city person, born in London, probably on 31 October 1795. His father, Thomas, managed the livery stables at the Swan and Hoop inn and his mother Frances appears to been an attractive and lively woman of 'singular Character'. His interest in words emerged early. A neighbour recalled that when he was beginning to talk, 'instead of answering questions put to him, he would always make a rhyme to the last word people said, and then laugh'. From 1803 to 1810, he attended the school of Rev. John Clarke in Enfield, where he received a broad education and became acquainted with Greek, Latin and French literature.

Like Blake, Keats combined a close acquaintance with suffering and a passion for the imagination.

He was apprenticed as a surgeon in 1810 and eventually became a student at Guy's Hospital and in 1816 was licensed to practise as an apothecary, a kind of cross between a pharmacist and doctor. However, he soon abandoned a medical career in favour of poetry.

His first published poem appeared in 1816 and the next two years saw the production of virtually all his poetic output.

Keats's letters reveal an extraordinarily intelligent and sensitive nature but although he may have declared that 'I find I cannot exist without poetry', the letters also reveal an engagingly witty, down-to-earth personality with a zest for life.

Sadly his life was beset with personal tragedy. His father died when he was eight. His mother died of tuberculosis when he was fourteen. In the winter of 1818 Keats tended his younger brother, Tom, who died in December, just a fortnight after his nineteenth birthday. At this time he fell deeply in love with Fanny Brawne, but a sore throat was already troubling him. In little over a year he was in the full grip of tuberculosis. Hoping to recover his health, in mid-September 1820, he set sail for 'the warm south' and on his twenty-fifth birthday he landed in Naples. Four months later, on 23 February 1821, he died in Rome.

from

ISABELLA; *OR* THE POT OF BASIL

Gothic horror and romance were very popular in Keats's day.

This poem tells the grisly story of two lovers in medieval Italy, Isabella and Lorenzo. All would be well, were it not that her two brothers consider Lorenzo to be too lowly born; they wish their sister to marry some noble worthy of their wealth. Consequently, they murder Lorenzo on a hunting trip and bury him in the forest. On returning, they inform Isabella that Lorenzo has gone abroad. Isabella is inconsolable until one night a vision of Lorenzo appears to her and reveals the truth. Isabella goes to the forest and uncovers the body and brings back Lorenzo's head which she keeps in a pot of basil.

Her brothers, curious why their sister should spend so much time over the now flourishing plant, steal it and discover the rotting head. Horrified, they flee the country, leaving Isabella insane and grieving over her stolen basil-pot.

This short extract presents a dramatically brief account of the fateful hunting trip.

COMMENT

Keats was always attracted by stories and legends from far away times and places. Here, like Shakespeare before him, he borrows from the famous fourteenth-century Italian writer Giovanni Boccaccio.

Keats was dissatisfied with the poem and, even in this short extract, it is possible to sense how the rather

bloodthirsty subject-matter does not sit well with the
verse form, also borrowed from the Italian and which
Keats uses rather awkwardly.

from
LAMIA   This long and elaborate poem tells of how a young
                         Corinthian philosopher, Lycius, falls in love with
                         the magical creature, Lamia, a snake granted human
                         form.

                         In this extract, Keats presents a succession of images of
                         the ancient city of Corinth at night which Lycius and
                         Lamia have just entered.

COMMENT   This is not a real city such as the one depicted in
                         Blake's 'London', but Keats demonstrates his skill at
                         creating an intensely compressed impression of activity
                         played out against shifting images (see Literary Terms)
                         of light and shade.

GLOSSARY   **corniced** Keats is referring to the shade cast by the overhanging
                         stonework decorating the upper edge of a classical building
                         such as a temple

from
THE EVE OF ST AGNES

                         It is helpful to see the two extracts in context, so a brief
                         summary of the intervening stanzas is provided.

Stanzas I–III   This prelude to the main narrative establishes the
                         atmosphere (see Literary Terms) and setting for the
                         story that follows.

The images of the   The poem begins in the 'bitter chill' of a winter's night
dead contrast with   outside a medieval castle. The Beadsman slowly shuffles
the festivities   from the frozen landscape into the chapel attached to
inside and the   the castle, passing the effigies of dead noble men and
passion of the   women lying silently on the cold tombs. He approaches
lovers.   an entrance to the castle and hears the faint sounds of
                         music and festivities within. But instead of entering, he

turns away to spend his dying hours praying for forgiveness.

[Stanzas IV–XXII]

As the Beadsman is left to his sad fate, the poet leads us from the cold outside into the warmth and splendour of a banquet in the castle.

Stanzas XXIII–XXV

Madeline, the daughter of the Baron, has left the banquet and arrives at her chamber, excited by the thought of conjuring up an image of her lover in her dreams. The effect of the moonlight illuminating the chamber's stained-glass window is described in detail. Here Keats produces a remarkable concentration of words that have associations of intense richness and colour.

As she prays, she is likened to an angel. The pale moonlight falling on her form produces a magical effect. Meanwhile, Porphyro, who loves Madeline but is hated by the Baron, has been smuggled into the bedchamber where he hides and watches. As she prays he is overwhelmed by her angelic beauty.

[Stanzas XXVI–XXXIX]

Porphyro emerges from his hiding-place and lays a feast of rich and exotic delicacies before the sleeping Madeline. He whispers to her to awake. As he serenades her with an ancient love song, she opens her eyes but still sees Porphyro as a marvellous dream. They declare their love but as the moon sets, reality breaks in and they must flee the castle to escape the cruel vengeance of 'dwarfish Hildebrand', the Baron.

Stanzas XL–XLII

Keats creates suspense by using details that are now familiar in horror films, etc.

The lovers make their way through the silent castle. Lamps flicker, tapestries flutter and carpets rise and fall in the draughts from the storm outside. As they reach the door, a guard dog stirs but, recognising Madeline, does not raise the alarm. Gradually the bolts are pulled, allowing the lovers to escape, leaving the occupants of the castle to their nightmares. The poem ends where it began, with the Beadsman, who after a lifetime of prayer, sleeps in his lonely grave.

COMMENT   The poem's narrative is organised around a number of recurring contrasts: cold/warmth, death/life, richness/poverty, youth/age, religious purity/physical desire, hatred/love, dream/reality, permanence/change.

The figures of the dying Beadsman, the virginal Madeline and the passionate Porphyro, the threat of the Baron, the richness of the window illuminated by the cool moonlight, the peace of the bedchamber, the storm raging outside, the escape into the night all contribute to the network of contrasts within the poem.

The use of terms drawn from heraldry ('device', 'emblazonings', 'scutcheon') maintains the medieval atmosphere.

Stanza XXIV is one of Keats's most famous descriptive passages and displays the poet's particularly concentrated way of combining words to achieve an intense appeal to the senses.

The elaborate richness of the window is skilfully offset by the more muted and purer tones of stanza XXV.

The final stanzas XL–XLII are built around tense movement (the lovers' stealthy descent, the fluttering tapestries, the wind outside, etc.) that contrasts not only with the sleeping castle, but with the magical stillness of Madeline's bedroom.

TO AUTUMN

Active terms, such as 'load', 'bend', 'fill', 'swell' and 'plump' stress the sense of excess.

In the first stanza the poet boldly evokes the richness of the season and the fullness of the harvest in all its aspects.

In a second stanza autumn is personified as a half-glimpsed, nymph-like figure haunting the harvest. This stanza has a more languorous air as the poet contemplates the intoxicating and almost dreamlike effects of the process of harvesting.

Words such as
'soft-dying',
'wailful', 'sinking',
'dies', introduce a
feeling of
melancholy.

The final stanza strikes a new, sadder note as the poet reflects upon the changing feelings that come with the passage of time. The optimism of spring has now been replaced in autumn by a sense of things coming to an end. But the poet finds comfort in the delicate fading of the season which has its own special beauty, reflected in a gentle evening landscape. The poem concludes with a symbol (see Literary Terms) of an end to the season – the departing swallows, and a symbol of the darker season to come – a newly arrived robin.

COMMENT

The poem is popularly famous for its celebration of abundance but, in fact, it is concerned not only with the pleasures of fulfilment, represented by autumn, but also with the question of impermanence, represented by changing seasons.

The poem is constructed like an arch: the process of fruition builds to a peak in the first two stanzas, and then drops away with thoughts on how the inevitability of change is a reminder of the impermanence of even the most intense pleasures.

In the second stanza the personification of autumn as a graceful nymph, reminiscent perhaps of the Lucy figure in 'A slumber did my spirit seal', lightens the texture and introduces a hint of movement.

The phrase '… the last oozings hours by hours' provides a culmination to the images evoking the richness of the harvest, but also introduces the notion of finality and change which is the subject of the last stanza.

The use of participle forms ('matur*ing*', 'gather*ing*', etc.) throughout the poem conveys a sense of *process* which is so important to Keats's theme.

ODE TO A NIGHTINGALE

Here, the poet reflects upon how the mysterious, unearthly song of the nightingale leads to a train of thoughts about the power of imagination, life and death.

Stanza 1

The poet establishes a sense of heady intoxication, as though he were drugged.

An exquisite mixture of pain and pleasure is established at the outset.

Stanza 2

Provence is also associated with medieval minstrels.

The poet is swept along by thoughts of rich wine and the warm, sunbaked landscape with which it is associated. So powerful are these thoughts that he wishes to escape the everyday world into the mysterious realm of the nightingale.

Stanza 3

This escape would leave far behind life's harsh realities. The nightingale knows nothing of the pain and suffering of life, where nothing, not even beauty, survives the ravages of time.

Stanza 4

The poet insists that he can indeed escape, not by resorting to wine, but through the power of poetry. In his imagination, he can join the nightingale in its strange, dark, romantic world.

Stanza 5

The poet has entered the nightingale's realm and in the darkness, although he cannot see, the scents of late spring and early summer envelop him.

Stanza 6

So intense is this moment of imagination, that the poet wishes that he could preserve it for ever, even dying while savouring the ecstasy of the nightingale's song at its peak. However, that would only serve to leave the nightingale chanting a funeral song over the dead poet.

Stanza 7

The nightingale is indeed immortal in the sense that the very song that touched the poet has been heard throughout history, reflecting both the sadness and joy of humanity. Like the poet, others have been led into the realms of the imagination and conjured up visions of romantic worlds.

Stanza 8   The nightingale's song begins to drift away and the poet is brought back to reality. The experience was so powerful, however, that he is uncertain whether he is awake or dreaming. He is left questioning whether the world of the imagination is the true reality.

COMMENT   As in Wordsworth's 'To A Skylark' or 'The Solitary Reaper', the image of the title is a spur to wider thoughts concerning the poet's state of mind. Essentially, the poem is built around a contrast between the poet's immediate capacity for the pleasures of the imagination, represented by his joy in the nightingale's song, and his awareness of the pain of life.

The opening words refer to a kind of drugged state of the kind that may be most commonly attained through alcohol, but for Keats is a product of his imagination, as exercised in poetry.

The death of the youth (line 26) may refer to Keats's brother, Tom.

The references to the fever and the fret, etc. are a reminder that, being a Londoner and trained in medicine, like Blake, he had seen physical suffering at close quarters.

In stanza 6 Keats wishes that it were possible to preserve his pleasure for ever by dying while it is at its height, but he knows that it is not possible; he is only 'half in love with easeful death'.

The feeling of sadness suggested by 'forlorn' is also found in Wordsworth's poetry.

Stanza 7 reflects on immortality and those feelings which outlive the individuals who experience them. The nightingale becomes a symbol (see Literary Terms) for art and the force of the imagination, which offer a kind of immortality for the individual who, like Keats, must return to reality. Like all earthly things the nightingale passes on.

THEMES, LANGUAGE & STYLE

Keats is probably most famous for his ability to evoke
scenes of sensuous intensity. Keats himself once wished
for 'a life of sensations'. Compared with Wordsworth or
Blake, Keats is much more concerned with capturing in
detail the sense of actually experiencing a particular
moment.

For all his descriptive powers, Keats did not directly
depict the world about him. Instead he creates his own
imaginative worlds, whether medieval fantasies as in
Isabella or *The Eve of St Agnes* or the trance-like state of
'Ode to a Nightingale'.

At the core of Keats's poetry is the imagination. The
imagination is both the creative force behind the poems
and their subject. Throughout his life, the imagination
was like a drug to Keats. During medical lectures his
mind used to wander into those 'faery lands forlorn' to
which he refers in 'Ode to a Nightingale'.

He once wrote Keats was also acutely aware of personal suffering and
'This is the world 'the weariness, the fever and the fret'. Consequently,
– thus we cannot throughout Keats's poetry there is a tension between
expect to give way the power of the imagination to capture perfect joy and
many hours to the nature of life that decrees that nothing is
pleasure.' permanent, least of all our pleasure: Porphyro and
Madeline must flee into the brutal reality of the storm;
the nightingale moves on and the richness of autumn
gives way to winter.

No poet has used words more intensely than Keats, nor
achieved a more sustained richness of effect. Most
immediately distinctive is his ability to appeal to the
senses.

The most obvious technique is to use words as much
for their associations as for their surface meaning. The
first stanza of 'To Autumn' builds up a sense of fullness
this way.

Keats was also alert to the possibilities of concentrating feelings. He could, for example, describe one sense by using the language associated with another. In 'Ode to a Nightingale' he refers to wine *tasting* of '*Flora*' and '*country green*', '*Dance*', 'Provençal *song*', and '*sunburnt mirth*'. This device is known as synaesthesia (see Literary Terms) and in this quotation, Keats uses one example ('sunburnt *mirth*') within another.

Another technique is to combine words in flexible grammatical constructions so as to create more than one possible meaning. For example, 'moss'd cottage-trees' in 'To Autumn' seems at first to be a very precise phrase, until one asks what precisely is 'moss'd'. Is it the trees, or the cottage, or both? To what exactly does the phrase 'cottage-trees' refer? This creative ambiguity in some ways anticipates the techniques of Gerard Manley Hopkins.

A

Identify the poems from which these words are taken.

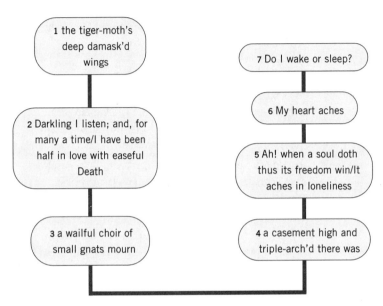

1 the tiger-moth's deep damask'd wings

2 Darkling I listen; and, for many a time/I have been half in love with easeful Death

3 a wailful choir of small gnats mourn

4 a casement high and triple-arch'd there was

5 Ah! when a soul doth thus its freedom win/It aches in loneliness

6 My heart aches

7 Do I wake or sleep?

Check your answers on page 96.

B

Consider these issues.

a How Keats employs contrast in *The Eve of St Agnes*.

b The ways in which Keats is able to appeal to all the senses in his descriptions.

c The contrast between the desire to seek pleasure and everyday reality.

d Keats's skill in creating his 'faery lands' either by setting his poems in distant times and places or by presenting his own dream world.

e The various ways in which pleasure and pain or joy and sadness are combined.

GERARD MANLEY HOPKINS (1844–89)

BACKGROUND

Hopkins was born in Stratford, Essex, the eldest of nine children. His parents had a deep interest in the arts; his father had published poetry and two of his brothers became professional artists.

Catholic influence

He went to Highgate School and, in 1863, on to Balliol College, Oxford, where he gained a first-class degree. At Oxford he came under the influence of prominent scholars and churchmen who wished the Anglican Church, to which the Hopkins family belonged, to rejoin the Roman Catholic Church.

In 1866 he was received into the Catholic Church and two years later decided to become a Jesuit priest.

The next few years were largely devoted to study (including learning Welsh) until in 1876 he wrote 'The Wreck of the Deutschland', inspired by the loss at sea of five Franciscan nuns. The poem was regarded as too difficult.

Undismayed, he continued to write some of his best known poetry at this time, including 'Pied Beauty'.

After his ordination as a priest, he worked in several industrial parishes including Liverpool in 1880–81. 'Felix Randall' and 'Spring and Fall' were written at this time.

Academia

After a spell at Catholic colleges, in 1884 he was appointed Professor of Greek and Latin at University College, Dublin, but he found the burden of work too demanding and he became deeply depressed and physically ill. Much of his poetry at this time reflects his dark mood.

He recovered briefly but died of typhoid in June 1889.

Posthumous recognition

Most of Hopkins's work did not gain public attention until the poet, Robert Bridges, who had been his friend since their Oxford days, published a volume of his

Poems in 1918. At the time, his writing was considered 'strange'. Even today, it presents difficulties, but Hopkins has come to be regarded as one of the most original and inventive nineteenth-century poets; his work can convey with unique directness the excitement of being alive and the beauty of creation, but can also plumb the depths of personal despair and self-doubt.

His poems

Hopkins's poetry is particularly difficult to summarise because he rarely describes or gives an account in a conventional way. Nevertheless, his poems are based on acute observation and he selects and combines words with great precision, so as to create a *verbal equivalent* of the scene or situation he is presenting. For the new reader this may be a rather difficult technique to grasp, but it may be helpful to remember that Hopkins had shown considerable talent as an artist and he always saw things with an artist's eye. When portraying a scene, the artist records images that occur *simultaneously* – there is no beginning or ending to a picture, even though it has a design and structure. Hopkins tries to do something similar in his poetry, so that, as far as possible, the *wholeness* of the situation is captured. Furthermore, unlike the painter who can deal only with visual images, Hopkins was able to extend this principle to his handling of thoughts and emotions.

INVERSNAID

The whole body of the poem is run through with rhymes (see Literary Terms) and near rhymes.

In the first stanza the poet presents a stream rushing down a mountainside until, in the second stanza, it forms a waterfall pouring into a dark pool. By the third stanza the stream flows more gently as it laps the plants on its banks.

In the fourth stanza the poet rejoices in all the properties of the stream and the unspoilt nature of which it is the essence.

COMMENT   The compression of words conveying different properties into a single phrase ('rollrock', 'windpuff-bonnet', 'fell-frowning') is a distinctive feature of Hopkins's poetry.

Commentators have noted that in his journals, Hopkins frequently made closely observed comparisons ('like fat', 'like green lettering', etc.) but that in his poetry he cleans out conventional constructions and searches for a more exact verbal equivalent, so as to create a more intense involvement with his subject. Hence, 'fell-frowning' rather than 'frowning like a fell'.

HEAVEN-HAVEN: A NUN TAKES THE VEIL

The poem is an extended metaphor (see Literary Terms). The nun who is about to enter the convent looks forward to a haven of peace and tranquillity away from the storms of everyday life.

COMMENT   This is an early poem, written during Hopkins's days at Oxford. Phrases such as 'the swing of the sea', show that Hopkins was already seeking to capture the physical force of natural features.

FELIX RANDALL

The poet recalls how, as a priest, he helped one of his parishioners.

First stanza: The physical and mental decline is recorded of a man who was once the image of manliness and strength.

Second stanza: The poet explains that he was able to offer spiritual comfort to a man who was unable to come to terms with his serious illness.

Third stanza: The poet expresses satisfaction at the comfort he was able to offer. Not only was the priest able to help the dying man but, in return, he gained

Think what images of the man are combined in the phrase 'hardy-handsome'.

personal strength from an experience which touched him deeply. For him, Felix Randall is a vulnerable child.

Final stanza: The poet reflects on how different Felix Randall was in his prime, when with all his strength as a working blacksmith, he could have no thought of what he would become.

COMMENT

This poem belongs to the time that Hopkins served as a priest in Liverpool.

The satisfaction that Hopkins feels at helping the blacksmith contrasts strongly with the despair registered in 'My own heart …'.

The poem is in four parts: the first (lines 1–4) depicts the spiritual decline of the giant of a man; the second (lines 5–8) recalls his spiritual recovery ending with a prayer for his soul's rest; the third (9–11) reflects on how Hopkins is spiritually richer for the experience; the concluding lines declare respect and gratitude for Felix Randall's former physical prowess, which may be seen to complement his later spiritual strength.

GLOSSARY

farrier a blacksmith who specialised in shoeing horses

mended got better

and all as well (dialect)

all road even if (dialect)

drayhorse a large horse used for pulling heavy carts

sandal horseshoe

SPRING AND FALL: TO A YOUNG CHILD

Note how the different meanings of 'spring' and 'fall' help us to understand the poem.

This tender poem is a concentrated and complex reflection on youth and age, innocence and experience. It addresses a little girl whose innocent and heartfelt response to the changes in the seasons seems to contrast with the poet's own, more knowing awareness.

Lines 1–4 show the child's genuine sadness at the

Y

falling leaves. Her feelings are unspoilt by other considerations.

Lines 4–8 compare the girl's present response with how it will be as an adult. She will have become indifferent to the withered leaves as such, but she will be sad because she knows what they signify.

The argument then turns in on itself, to suggest that, although the child does not yet know why she is grieving, all grief, whether innocent or not, has the same origin, namely, human mortality as a result of original sin. In this respect, the child is no different from the adult, so that, in effect Margaret in all her innocence is grieving for her own mortality.

COMMENT   The poem depends on the interweaving of two underlying ideas:
- Children in the 'spring' of life have a natural innocence, as yet uncorrupted by experience
- We are all 'fallen' as a result of the original sin committed by Adam and Eve in the Garden of Eden

By definition, the young girl is 'fallen' but that does not prevent Hopkins from finding a sad beauty in the girl's innocent grieving over the fallen leaves, an image which in turn becomes a reflection of the sadness of humanity.

GLOSSARY   **blight** curse

SPRING

Compare the techniques and effects in this poem to those in 'Pied Beauty' and 'The Starlight Night'.

The first eight lines (the octave) of this sonnet present a vivid series of flashing images (see Literary Terms) in which new growth, birdsong, blossom and new-born lambs seem to combine in ceaseless movement.

The last six lines (the sestet – see Literary Terms) give meaning to all this richness. The language is quite difficult but the sense seems to be that the scene just

Like Keats,
Hopkins is aware
of the short-lived
nature of the
season.

described is a kind of distillation or 'strain' of the purity of the Garden of Eden. That being the case, he prays that Christ should accept this innocence before it is lost. What is dedicated to Christ seems to be both the innocence of the young, symbolised (see Literary Terms) by the spring, and the innocent joy that is created from glorying in God's creation.

COMMENT

This celebratory poem offers an interesting contrast to the more muted feelings of 'Spring and Fall'.

The force of Hopkins's enthusiasm is conveyed in the unceremonious directness of his prayer: 'Have, get, before it cloy …'.

PIED BEAUTY

The 'trades' may
bring Felix
Randall to mind.

This short poem is an ecstatic celebration of the glory of God's creation in all its variety and oddity. The first stanza presents a stream of examples of 'pied' things, which are drawn from diverse aspects of creation, including the trades of man.

The second stanza sums up, as it were, the essence of 'dappledness' in opposites of different kinds, relating to colour, taste, speed and brightness. God should be praised because it is He who was able to make such contradictions and contrasts part of the unity of creation.

COMMENT

The poem comprises a mere seventy-nine words, some of which are combinations, yet they seem to suggest a tremendous variety of features and effects.

The poem may be usefully compared to the opening stanza of Keats's 'To Autumn' which also seeks to convey more than can be indicated specifically. Keats's phrase 'moss'd cottage-trees' in some ways anticipates Hopkins's technique.

The variousness of creation is mimicked in the second stanza by presenting strings of words in startling combinations.

GLOSSARY   **dappled** irregularly spotted
                stipple painted in dots or flashes of colour
                fold land enclosed for livestock
                fallow land left unsown

BINSEY POPLARS: FELLED 1879

Hopkins's artist's eye is very much to the fore here.

This straightforward, but sensitive poem, expresses a sense of physical, emotional and spiritual loss.

The first part is a lament for the poplars themselves. The poet recreates a sense of their trembling delicacy and how they were an essential element of the riverside scene.

The second part is a lament for mankind who abuses the 'especial' and fragile quality of nature. In the name of progress, we 'mend' but in reality we damage and 'unselve' the essential qualities of a scene for ever.

COMMENT   It is not only the outward beauty of the scene that Hopkins feels for, but its unity and inner integrity. This 'especial' quality of a thing, Hopkins sometimes referred to as 'inscape'.

GLOSSARY   **aspens** another word for the poplar tree
                airy cages light foliage
                seeing ball eye
                unselve destroy essential character or identity

THE STARLIGHT NIGHT

The sense of amazement reminds us of Blake's 'Tyger'.

The first part of this sonnet (see Literary Terms) is a series of exclamations celebrating God's creation. With childlike wonder, he discerns a whole world in the skies which, in its intense and glittering way, mirrors and complements scenes on earth. Such a vision is a prize worth seizing.

In the second part the poet asks with what can this prize be purchased. The answer comes that it is with prayer and devotion. Armed with that thought, the poem ends with a return to a vision of the heavens as a gloriously shining estate in spring, which is home to Christ, Mary and all his angels.

COMMENT   The poem maintains a sense of overwhelming astonishment at the beauty of creation.

The sense of wonder is conveyed in part by Hopkins's assumption of a childlike, open-eyed view of the stars, which invests them with life and activity.

Hopkins also revitalises the notion of the 'heavens' as the home of God.

GLOSSARY   **citadel** city fortress

             abele the white poplar tree

IN THE VALLEY OF THE ELWY

The poet remembers the kindly but undeserved treatment he once received when visiting friends. Their kindness seemed to be reflected in their oneness with their beautiful surroundings which offer them a kind of benevolent protection.

See if there are any similarities or differences between Hopkins's and Thomas's feelings about the Welsh.

The Welsh countryside and all its features are equally beautiful but the Welsh are unlike his friends; there is not the same sympathy between the environment and its people.

The poem concludes with a prayer that God should repair the Welsh people's deficiencies.

COMMENT   The key idea in this poem is that of a 'correspondence' between mankind and the natural beauty of God's

Y

creation. There was an accord between the kind people in the first part and their natural surroundings, which afforded them a protective 'hood'. In the case of 'the world of Wales' one can only pray that the 'creature', man and nature together, will be 'complete'.

Related ideas hinging on Hopkins's belief in the wholeness of creation are expressed in 'Spring', 'Pied Beauty', 'Binsey Poplars', 'The Starlight Night' and 'Felix Randall'.

GLOSSARY   **cordial** reviving

MY OWN HEART LET ME MORE HAVE PITY ON

This sonnet (see Literary Terms) was written in a state of deep depression but explores the possibility of relief.

Note what images suggest Hopkins's helplessness. In the first part he urges himself to turn his priestly pity on his own suffering and allow his heart time to recover. As it is, his depression makes the search for comfort as fruitless as the blind searching for life.

In the second part he goads himself to give comfort a chance to grow in God's time. The relief will not come through forcing but only by admitting those unforeseen moments that strike one such as a sudden glimpse of natural beauty.

COMMENT   See Comment for next poem.

THOU ART INDEED JUST, LORD ...

Hopkins instructed that the poem should be read quite slowly and with great rhythm (see Literary Terms). This sonnet (see Literary Terms), written in Hopkins's last year of life is in a far more direct style than most of his verse. The poet expresses his bitterness that sinners should prosper while he is engulfed in despair and a sense of failure. It could be no worse if God were his enemy. He sees about him the idle and unworthy prospering while he is barren.

In the second part, the poet turns to his usual source of inspiration, the natural world. It is spring and the world is rebuilding, but not the poet; the creative impulse has deserted him; Time has sapped his power. He is left to pray that his God will water the roots of his soul and imagination so that it will grow again.

COMMENT   These last two poems date from Hopkins's final years when he was plunged into deep depression. If the poems of his happiest years celebrate the positive evidence of his faith in God, his last poems are concerned with finding his God again in the face of personal despair.

Hints of a darker side to Hopkins's vision were already evident in 'Spring and Fall', in which a shadow is cast over childhood innocence.

Broadly speaking, 'My Own Heart ...' is concerned with Hopkins's loss of spiritual strength, whilst 'Thou art indeed just, Lord ...' dwells on his loss of creative powers.

Hopkins's sense of impoverished imagination is suggested in the last poem by the fact that the poet's distinctively energetic and original word-formations are, as it were, almost entirely stripped away, to produce a much plainer text.

Hopkins's characteristic dance-like rhythm (see Literary Terms) so evident in poems like 'Pied Beauty' has been replaced in 'Thou art indeed just, Lord' by a more solemn tread.

THEMES, LANGUAGE & STYLE

Like Blake, Hopkins was concerned with the wholeness of creation, but since Blake's day, science had uncovered much more about the complexity and diversity of the natural world. For some, the developments in geology and evolutionary theory called Biblical truth and religious faith into question. Hopkins himself was an enthusiastic observer and until his last dark days at least, the more that could be seen, the more awe-struck and excited he became about God's creation.

Consequently, Hopkins's poetry is crammed with details, not only of physical features, but with phrases capturing movement and how the living world fits together.

The energy of Hopkins's poetry derives not only from his original descriptive powers but from the sound and construction of his verse. Most famously, Hopkins developed what he called sprung rhythm. Essentially, sprung rhythm is based on the natural stresses (see rhythm in Literary Terms) of speech patterns, rather than a regular alternation of stressed and unstressed syllables.

The effect is best illustrated by comparing two sonnets (see Literary Terms). Wordsworth's 'Composed upon Westminster Bridge' employs regular ten-syllable lines and, in theory at least, has a regular pattern of five stressed syllables per line. By comparison, 'Felix Randall' is much more flexible and there is no limit on the number of syllables in a line but there are some very obvious stresses. Try reading them aloud; it is just about possible to read the Wordsworth in a regular sing-song voice, but the Hopkins resists such treatment. You may note that the stresses are often brought about by the frequent use of alliteration (see Literary Terms).

A *Identify the poems from which these words are taken.*

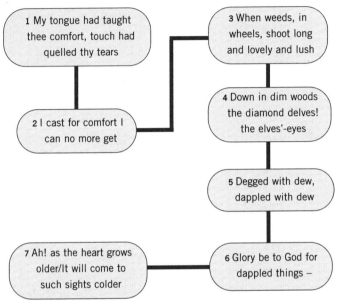

1 My tongue had taught thee comfort, touch had quelled thy tears

3 When weeds, in wheels, shoot long and lovely and lush

2 I cast for comfort I can no more get

4 Down in dim woods the diamond delves! the elves'-eyes

5 Degged with dew, dappled with dew

7 Ah! as the heart grows older/It will come to such sights colder

6 Glory be to God for dappled things –

Check your answers on page 96.

B *Consider these issues.*

a The ways in which Hopkins demonstrates the unity of God's creation.

b How Hopkins expresses the joy of being alive.

c The ways in which the poet uses precisely observed details in his poetry.

d The ways in which Hopkins is able to combine words in unusual ways.

e Hopkins's individual use of stress, alliteration and rhyme (see Literary Terms) to give much of his poetry its characteristic energy.

T. S. ELIOT (1888–1965)

BACKGROUND

Thomas Stearns Eliot was born in St Louis, Missouri. His father was a businessman from a well-known East Coast family.

In 1906 he entered Harvard University, gaining his BA degree in 1909 and his MA in 1911. During 1910–11 he attended lectures at the Sorbonne in Paris. He returned to Europe in 1914 as a travelling fellow in philosophy at Merton College, Oxford.

A change of nationality

His Oxford career did not last, however, but he decided to remain in England and only very occasionally did he return to the country of his birth; he became a British subject in 1927.

In 1915 he embarked on an unhappy marriage to Vivien Haigh-Wood, an English girl from a conventional and well-to-do family. This experience undoubtedly contributed to the sense of emptiness that is found in much of his work.

For a while he worked as a schoolmaster in High Wycombe and Highgate, then joined the colonial and foreign department of Lloyd's Bank.

Recognition as a poet

Whilst pursuing his professional duties at the bank, he continued his writing and by the end of the First World War, he was establishing his reputation as a poet. His first volume of verse, *Prufock and other Observations*, appeared in 1917, followed by *Poems* in 1919. He was also making his mark as a literary critic and his first volume of criticism, *The Sacred Wood*, appeared in 1920.

In 1922 Eliot published *The Waste Land* which quickly established itself as the classic modern text.

In 1925 he became a director of publishing house, Faber & Faber, where he was influential in the development of a succession of now famous English poets.

For the next thirty years Eliot continued to write poems, plays and criticism on a wide variety of literature, although he wrote little poetry in his later years.

His first wife died in 1947 and he married Valerie Fletcher in 1957. He was awarded the Nobel Prize for Literature and Order of Merit in 1948 and was recognised as England's most distinguished man of letters.

Establishment figure

Unlike Blake, but in some ways like Wordsworth, Eliot became an establishment figure in his later years, after his ground-breaking earlier work. More than any other poet he created a style of poetic writing that we recognise as distinctly modern, and few contemporary poets would not admit to being influenced by his work in some way or other.

PRELUDES
Poem I

This poem presents a series of images of an early winter's evening in a city during the early years of this century. The details all suggest desolation and although a city is a place for people, no human beings are represented, only the effects of their activity.

Poem II

'Vacant' is a key word. Think what meanings it can have.

This poem represents the dingy after-effects of the previous evening's activities, the 'smell of steaks' is replaced by 'stale smells of beer' and the 'lonely cab-horse' has given way to the busy 'sawdust-trampled street'. The new day begins but is seen as a pretence, as one considers all those anonymous citizens beginning the day in exactly the same drab, mechanical way.

Poem III

This poem addresses an individual woman, but she remains a faceless representative of urban squalor. She has a restless night in which images of her impoverished existence trouble her mind. The morning finds her clutching herself in sordid isolation from those passing in the street below, who know and care nothing of her existence.

Poem IV   The soul of modern man is bound up in the tawdry never-ending routine of city life which possesses an inescapable predictability.

The poet muses briefly on the sadness of such an existence but is himself tainted by the cynicism of modern life and turns away in laughter.

The reference to We are left with a picture image (see Literary Terms)
'vacant lots' of old women scouring waste land for fuel, possibly
returns us to the newspapers, to warm their lives, an image which sums
beginning. up the emptiness of modern life.

COMMENT   The title, 'Preludes', is in part ironic (see Literary Terms), as the poems turn in on themselves, with the implication that nothing follows but a repetition of what has gone before. A prelude may also be a short, self-standing piece of music.

The poems are arranged in a rotating time sequence: evening – morning – night to morning – evening to morning.

Such glimpses of people the poet offers are fragmentary and inseparable from the sordidness of the environment.

The disconnected nature of city life is partly reflected in the use of rhyme. The poet skilfully gives the impression that the rhymes appear almost by chance. There is a mixture of masculine rhymes ('wraps'/'scraps') and feminine rhymes ('shutters'/'gutters') – see rhyme in Literary Terms. Some words rhyme in couplets, others are widely spaced, even across stanzas. Some are partial rhymes ('skies'/'certainties'), others involve different rhythmical stress ('consciousness'/'press') – see rhythm in Literary

Terms. Some words do not rhyme at all. The rhyming words also suggest some curious connections of the sort that a city would throw up.

GLOSSARY   **curled the papers** Eliot is referring to long strips of paper wound around the hair, often left in overnight, in order to produce ringlets

MORNING AT THE WINDOW

The word 'tear'
suggests the
reluctance to make
even eye-contact.

The poet, looking from a window, records his impressions of a street, looking down at the basement kitchens where housemaids toil at their daily chores, occasionally looking up and catching the embarrassed eye of passers-by.

COMMENT   This poem explores similar territory to that of 'Preludes' – the emptiness of city life with its sense of alienation.

GLOSSARY   **area** space below ground level, between basement and street

JOURNEY OF THE MAGI

One of the Magi, or wise men, describes the journey to Bethlehem.

The first section paints a picture in some considerable

Eliot deliberately paints a picture that seems to have nothing to do with religious belief.

detail of their difficulties: the harsh weather conditions, the reluctant camels, the indiscipline of the camels' handlers, the numerous discomforts and the hostilities they met on the way. Eventually they decided to travel light but, all the time, they thought of the comforts of home and questioned whether the journey was really worth the effort.

Judas betrayed Christ for thirty pieces of silver!

The second section describes the approach to their destination. They call at an inn, where men are gambling for some pieces of silver, and make enquiries but with no success. After the extensive account of the journey, the section ends abruptly, merely recording that finally they arrived. No further information is given other than the bald statement that what they found was 'satisfactory'.

See if there are any similarities between the speaker's unease and the feelings expressed in other poems.

The final section is a reflection on the significance of their discovery. Despite the hardship, the speaker would do the same journey again but, even after the lapse of time, he is disturbed by what he saw. In the normal course of human affairs, birth and death are seen as distinct events, but this birth was somehow different. It was undoubtedly a birth but at the same time it signified death – the death of all the Magi had stood for.

They returned to their kingdoms but felt like strangers in a foreign land and could no longer hold any belief in their traditional gods. Tired of life, the narrator would find his own death a relief.

COMMENT

'Journey of the Magi' was published in the same year, 1927, that Eliot became a British subject and a member of the Church of England. From this time, his writing was much concerned with religious matters and he came to the view that the tradition of the Christian Church was the answer to the fragmentation of modern society.

The experiences of the Magi with rebellious drivers, extortionate prices and general discomfort are representative of the urban greed and squalor that Eliot had charted in poems such as 'Preludes'.

RANNOCH, BY GLENCOE

The poem is a reflection upon a remote landscape which, for all its calmness and the dreamlike way in which the land and the sky seem to blend into one, still seems to hold the memory of the massacre that once took place here. The winding road which leads up into the Pass at Glencoe draws the poet into thoughts of the confusion of battle and the memory of the broken pride that still lingers.

COMMENT   See under next poem.

USK

The poet seems to be suggesting that, however much we may wish to rediscover ancient legends and beliefs associated with the landscape, we must view it in the light of our own faith and values. We should not read into the landscape that which is not our own.

COMMENT   These two elusive poems dwell on the idea that landscapes hold memories but hint that, while they may stimulate and guide our thoughts ('The road winds' – 'the roads dip'), mankind must settle its own affairs.

A COOKING EGG

The name 'Pipit' suggests something birdlike and lightweight.

The first two stanzas present a scene of sterility and faded youth as the narrator sits observing Pipit framed by mementos of her past.

The central section is a kind of parody (see Literary Terms) of a heavenly vision of fulfilment. The opening line of each stanza emphasises how in his life he has failed to achieve fame, money, social recognition and personal love.

The final section expresses his personal disillusion and sense of the impoverishment of modern life, in which all aspirations are stifled by sordid small-mindedness.

COMMENT

This poem shows Eliot at his most cynical. It may well reflect the desperate unhappiness of his first marriage. However, whatever personal feeling may lie behind it, Eliot is commenting on the emptiness and triviality of modern life in general.

The second stanza is a wicked parody (see Literary Terms) of the 23rd Psalm with its repetition of the words 'I shall not want ...'. The echo of the psalmists' song calls to mind thoughts of raising one's eyes heavenwards, but the narrator's thoughts are decidedly earthly. The rag-bag of persons he shall meet in Heaven represents the confusion of moral and spiritual values of which Eliot was so critical. The narrator's only answer to a perverted existence is to seek other perversions.

See if Eliot's London has anything in common with the city in 'Preludes'.

The final section is a bitter condemnation of the stifling and inescapable narrowness of modern urban existence. There is a fleeting glimpse of wider horizons (the reference to eagles and trumpets hints at heroic aspirations, possibly those of Coriolanus), but it is immediately stifled, and the poem ends in anti-climax.

GLOSSARY

Sir Philip Sidney a sixteenth-century scholar, poet and courtier, regarded by some as the perfect man

Coriolanus a famous Roman general who was flawed by his arrogance

Sir Alfred Mond the wealthy founder of Imperial Chemical Industries

Lucretia Borgia a famous patron of the arts in sixteenth-century Italy but associated with murder, intrigue and incest

Y

Madame Blavatsky Russian mystic and co-founder of
Theosophy, condemned as a fraud by the Society for Psychical
Research
Piccarda de Donati a spiritual guide from Dante's *Inferno*
Kentish Town, Golder's Green areas of London

TRIUMPHAL MARCH

A march in honour of an unnamed dictator is seen
through the eyes of ordinary onlookers.

*Think what effect
on you the
introduction of the
subject of sausages
has.*

The first section sets the scene. Crowds are gathering
in anticipation of the great march. The traditional
images and emblems of triumphal show, 'stone, bronze,
stone, steel, etc.' impress themselves on the mind.
Sustained by their sausages, the onlookers wait, until, at
last, the march-past comes into sight.

A demonstration of the dictator's military might slowly
passes by.

Eventually the display of arms has moved on to be
followed by loyal civic dignitaries and representatives of
all aspects of society. Finally the dictator, the supreme
ruler, comes into sight. The observers are surprised that
he appears to show no emotion or reveal any
personality.

*Notice what idea
the reference to
dust introduces.*

The procession has passed and makes its way towards
the temple to prepare for the sacrificial rituals. The
account of the march ends as it began, with the symbols
of triumph, to which is added 'dust'.

The final section is a kind of epilogue. The march is
over. All that remains is an impression of the pomp.

*The 'crumpets', a
pun on trumpets,
remind us of the
depressing end of
'A Cooking Egg'.*

Thoughts turn to humbler matters: the visit to church,
Cyril's confusion of the church bell with that of a
street-crier, the uneaten sausage. The request for a light
for one's cigarette seems to become a desire for
illumination and help, but none is offered.

Y

COMMENT   The poem has obvious connections with the rise of
           militaristic and authoritarian regimes during the early
           years of the twentieth century. However, modern-day
           references to armaments and golf clubs, etc. merge with
           more traditional images (see Literary Terms), especially
           those associated with ancient Rome.

           The dictator is anonymous and without personality; the
           pursuit of power defines his being.

           The references to the symbols (see Literary Terms) of
           enduring power with which the poem begins are
           supplemented in the fourth section by dust, the symbol
           of mortality.

           The poem ends in anti-climax . The grandeur of the
           march has been reduced to thoughts of crumpets,
           sausages and a cigarette. The pomp and ceremony
           evaporates into a few fragments of conversation.

GLOSSARY   **Ego** an inflated sense of self-importance, but Eliot is thinking
            of the strict psychological term referring to that part of the
            mind relating to conscious awareness and perception

MACAVITY: THE MYSTERY CAT

           Macavity is a shabby, thieving, streetwise mongrel cat,
           who is blamed for everything, but has a habit of
           disappearing whenever there's trouble.

COMMENT   Although supposedly written as relaxation, Eliot's
           light-hearted cat poems display a mental agility and
           verbal dexterity that is to be found in all his best
           poetry.

           Much of the fun of the poem derives from the constant
           alternation between the image of the master criminal
           and the image of a cat; sometimes, as in lines 11–16,
           the human and feline qualities merge.

The reader may also be amused by the absurd contrasts between affairs of state and the affairs of a cat. A Foreign Office treaty has gone missing but so has the milk!

GLOSSARY   feline to do with cats
               depravity immorality, corruption

THEMES, LANGUAGE & STYLE

In many respects, Eliot's personal journey was the reverse of Hopkins's. Hopkins ended his life in despair, while Eliot's creative life began with a singularly bleak view of a rootless and purposeless humanity. In later life, however, Eliot took comfort in the Anglican Church because it offered him a continuing link with tradition, which he felt modern life had so nearly severed. The contrast is seen most clearly by comparing 'A Cooking Egg' with 'Journey of the Magi'.

Eliot was most influential in his verse forms, which more than any other previous English poet broke with the formalities of traditional poetry. It is his ability to follow the contours of a thinking mind, and his readiness to jump in unpredictable directions, that led to him being hailed as the first truly twentieth-century poet. 'Triumphal March' with its mixture of street conversation, lists of armaments, references to pomp and ritual and snippets of French, together with its sudden changes of pace and widely varying line lengths, is perhaps the clearest example in this selection.

Identify the poems from which these words are taken.

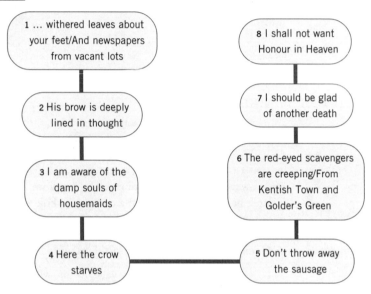

1 ... withered leaves about your feet/And newspapers from vacant lots

2 His brow is deeply lined in thought

3 I am aware of the damp souls of housemaids

4 Here the crow starves

5 Don't throw away the sausage

6 The red-eyed scavengers are creeping/From Kentish Town and Golder's Green

7 I should be glad of another death

8 I shall not want Honour in Heaven

Check your answers on page 96.

B **Consider these issues.**

a In 'Preludes', what use the poet makes of the passage of time.

b The aspects of city life that Eliot dislikes.

c How Eliot's uses anti-climax to suggest the pointlessness and triviality of modern life.

d The ways Eliot gains and keeps the reader's interest in 'Journey of the Magi'.

e The ways in which Eliot introduces unusual references and details into his poetry.

f Eliot's 'people' seem cut off from one another and communicate little. This isolation is very different from Wordsworth's solitariness.

Robert Frost (1874–1963)

Background

Early days

Frost was born in San Francisco but, when he was ten, on the death of his father, he moved with his mother and sister to the farming country of Massachusetts, near to his paternal grandparents.

In 1892 he entered Dartmouth College but soon left to return home where he taught in a school and worked in a variety of jobs in factories and on a local newspaper.

In 1894 he sold his first poem 'My Butterfly' and went on a perilous expedition into Virginia's swampland. The next year, he married Elinor Miriam White, a fellow graduate of Lawrence High School.

Farm life

After a spell at Harvard University, he settled with his family on a farm in New Hampshire. Although his experiences at this time deeply affected his poetry, he was not particularly successful, so he took up a number of teaching posts. By now the Frosts had produced six children, of whom two died in infancy.

In 1912, like his contemporary T.S. Eliot, he sailed for England, where his poetry was well received by some of the poets of the day. His first volumes of poetry were published at this time.

On the outbreak of the First World War, he returned to the United States, where his fame was spreading in the literary world of the East Coast.

He was able to purchase a farm, the first of many, in New Hampshire, but by now he had become a considerable literary figure and much of the remainder of his long life was given over to teaching, giving poetry readings and accumulating honorary degrees.

Personal tragedies

While his public fame continued undimmed, between the wars he suffered a series of personal tragedies. In 1934, his youngest child died. Four years later, his wife died of a heart attack. His son committed suicide in 1940, while a daughter and his sister succumbed to mental disorders.

His last major volume of poetry, *The Witness Tree*, containing darker poems which reflected these tragedies, was published in 1942, but he continued to write and gave his last public reading in 1962.

MOWING

Characteristically, Frost is moved but is uncertain about the experience.

Alone with his thoughts as he cuts the hay, the poet ponders the whispering sound of the scythe. What message does it convey? Perhaps the scythe whispers because of the sun-baked stillness of the landscape. Whatever truth the mowing holds, it is not to do with idle fantasy but with the reality of the task which takes on a dreamlike quality as the scythe cuts through grass and flowers, occasionally disturbing a snake.

COMMENT

Both this poem and 'The Pasture' concern routine and inconsequential farming activities which, almost by definition, are the antithesis of the dramatic. Contemplation of such simple subjects is characteristic of much of Frost's poetry.

It is interesting to compare 'Mowing' to a poem such as Wordsworth's 'The Solitary Reaper'. Wordsworth finds a universal message in the reaper's song, but the scythe's 'whispers' contain no mystical messages beyond hinting at the 'mystery' of work itself.

MENDING WALL

The poet squares up to the task of repairing a boundary wall after the ravages of winter and the damage caused by the hunters who, although never caught, leave gaps where they have removed stones so that their dogs can reach the rabbits.

Frost humorously imagines the stones to have a mind of their own.

He meets his neighbour to survey the boundary between their properties. Together they set about the task of rebuilding the drystone wall, selecting the right-sized stone, and willing them to stay in place until they are secured. Their fingers are rough through handling the stones but fitting the wall together is like a game.

The poet goes on to wonder what the walls are for. His neighbour's pine trees don't need protection from his apple trees on the other side of the wall. Why, the poet asks, should walls make good neighbours, especially where they are not keeping apart each other's cows, for instance.

Think why the poet repeats his neighbour's words.

If he were building a completely new wall the poet would ask if it was really necessary and what it was intended to keep in or keep out, for it seems in the natural order of things that they are destined to collapse. He would like his neighbour to recognise this fact, but his neighbour simply continues with the rebuilding just as his father had done, content in the assurance that 'good fences make good neighbours'.

COMMENT

There is a characteristically dry humour to this poem; it would be impossible, for instance, to imagine Wordsworth exclaiming, as Frost does in the opening line, at the sheer cussedness of affairs that brings about the collapse of the walls.

Much of the effect of the poem comes from the combination of Frost's steady unrolling of the events of the day and his quizzical account of his neighbour's homespun philosophy of 'good fences'.

Even though Frost applies a wry logic to the necessity of boundary walls (they cannot separate non-existent cows!), the poem seems to suggest the importance of human regard for each other. The poet may feel superior to his neighbour's unquestioning acceptance of the task, but he refrains from voicing his feelings.

After apple-picking

The use of the repeated rhymes (see Literary Terms), 'well', 'fell', 'tell' seems to suggest drowsiness.

It is the end of the harvest season, the autumn frosts are setting in and the poet is weary of apple-picking. The sheet of ice which he cleared from the drinking trough in the morning seems like a magnifying glass to his obsessive dream of apples, for he has worked so hard, that he cannot free his mind of the appearance of the fruit, the feeling of the ladder-rung pressing into his instep, the swaying of the ladder against the tree or the roar of the apples as they are poured into the bins. Ironically (see Literary Terms), his exhaustion is the result of the successful harvest he had so looked forward to. Every one of the thousands of apples were handled individually, for if they fell to the ground they were consigned to the cider pile. No wonder he is exhausted with apple-picking and thoughts of apple-picking.

The poet is left wondering whether his sleep is something special like the woodchuck's hibernation, or plain human fatigue.

COMMENT   Frost presents a very different view of harvest from Keats in 'To Autumn'. Keats is an observer, but, as so often, Frost is a participant in what he describes.

Apple-picking is a totally absorbing and exhausting activity and the bulk of the poem systematically and unsentimentally records the physical and mental experience.

Frost suggests an almost trance-like state of exhaustion but he sets it against hard facts, such as breaking the ice or the ache of standing for hours on a ladder-rung.

The poet is tempted to believe in some special insight induced by his sleep but, as in 'Mowing', he withdraws at the last moment; it was more than likely an ordinary 'human sleep'.

GLOSSARY   **ladder-round** the rung of a ladder

AN OLD MAN'S WINTER NIGHT

The single word 'clomping' sums up the man's age and stubbornness.

On a frosty night, an old man, lamp in hand, visits his cellar. The world outside looks in, as it were, from the darkness. Unable to remember what he wanted, the old man disturbs the silence of his cellar once again by clomping back upstairs.

The shifting log, the only movement, emphasises the scene's remoteness.

Outside, the wider world has its own sounds of trees and branches. Alone and content with his own thoughts, the old man sits in his own small ring of light. The pale moonlight is left to light the snow and ice which covers his farm while the man sleeps.

The poet is left wondering how the solitary old man can cope, physically and mentally, with his wider responsibilities and surroundings.

COMMENT   This poem throws into sharp relief the recurrent notion in Frost's work that we are both part of our environment and separate from it. The farm buildings and the surrounding land, familiar territory by daylight, are an extension of the old man and yet on this bitter winter's night they are as an alien world.

We become the observer here, and the scene is made vivid by the adoption of an almost cinematographic movement from a broad external shot in the darkness to a close-up focus on the source of light.

The old man is not identified in any way, yet he becomes the embodiment of vulnerability, combined with a certain sturdy resilience.

BIRCHES

The poet reflects in detail upon how slender birch trees come to arch and bend. Normally they are so flexible that they spring back but the poet goes on to describe the effects of snow and frost, which can weigh the branches down so heavily, that they are left permanently bent.

Here, Frost brings together the facts and what we prefer to feel.

However, although the weight of the ice may be the true cause, the poet would prefer to imagine that the branches had been bent over by a boy swinging on them. Living far from the town, swinging on each of his father's birch trees was his only sport.

Think why filling a cup to the brim is an effective image to express the climber's feelings.

The poet continues by describing in detail how the boy would learn to climb to the highest branches, launch himself into the air and be carried to the ground.

Once the poet did the same and, in a sense, he would like to do so again. There are times when day-to-day living is as troublesome and irritating as struggling through a dense wood and to soar out of the undergrowth would seem a release. But the poet does not want to escape from the cares of life permanently, so just as the birch tree lifts you into the air but sets you down to earth again, there would be satisfaction in escape and in returning to where one properly belongs.

COMMENT

Frost provides a seamless combination of direct observation, recollection and reflection, so that the whole poem comprises the gradual unravelling of the poet's thought processes. His observation of external nature seems effortlessly to match the workings of his mind.

Despite its easy flow, the poem has at its heart a tension between ascent and descent. The birches may be bent towards the earth but they may also carry us skywards. In the same way, the human spirit may inhabit the earth and everyday things but needs at times to soar heavenwards, if only eventually to return.

The poem wears its 'moral' lightly ('One could do worse…'), although there is a simple gravity in Frost's thoughts on life. The 'truths' about the behaviour of the birch trees and the solitary child becoming 'a swinger of birches' are as compelling as what the poet sees as their significance.

Two look at two

Think what details contribute to the sense that the lovers' walk seems to be approaching an anti-climax.

In failing light, two lovers near the end of their walk up a mountainside. To go further would be dangerous, but before they turn back, they peer over a broken-down wall at where they might have gone. All is silent and still. There is nothing to see and they turn away from the woods. But, suddenly, they see a female deer emerge from the wood and survey them from the other side of the wall. Having confirmed the two humans were no threat the deer moves on.

How is the title 'Two look at two' illustrated in the detail of the narrative?

Once again, the walk seems over, when a male deer comes into view and scrutinises them as if to challenge them to move and show that they are alive. Then the buck follows the doe along the wall.

The lovers are left alone, overwhelmed by the experience and feeling that nature, in the form of the two deer, has somehow presented them a mirror image of their love.

COMMENT   Frost intertwines the facts of a rare chance event and
           the magical feelings it engenders. The lovers *feel*
           enriched and confirmed in their love by nature's 'favour'
           although, characteristically, Frost makes no claim that
           the earth possesses any consciousness or sense of
           purpose.

           As in 'Birches', the force of the poem lies in the
           compelling immediacy of the occurrence and the steady,
           step-by-step presentation of events. The exact details
           such as the 'barbed-wire binding' or the 'jerks of the
           head' provide a vivid focus.

           As so often in his poetry, Frost seems to suggest that
           the natural and human worlds should live in some sort
           of equilibrium at those points at which they come into
           contact.

TREE AT MY WINDOW

COMMENT   The poet feels a physical and imaginative connection
           between the tree and himself. The tree has no message
           but the poet reflects upon the way outward nature, in
           the form of the tree, may be seen to mirror man's inner
           nature.

GLOSSARY   **diffuse** ill-defined

UNHARVESTED

COMMENT   The chance discovery of an apple tree that had dropped
           all its rich crop in a sweet-smelling ring of red, leads
           the poet to celebrate the unplanned things in life.

THE SILKEN TENT

COMMENT   This poem from a later period in Frost's career exhibits
           a more outwardly intellectual approach to composition
           than that represented by the conversational poems on
           rural subjects.

The poem is a sonnet (see Literary Terms), itself a disciplined and demanding verse form, and is constructed around an elaborate series of analogies. That is, the individual features of a tent are found systematically to correspond with aspects of a woman's character. The comparison is, to say the least, unusual, if not far-fetched, and it may be said that Frost is, in a way, imitating seventeenth-century 'metaphysical' poets who delighted in finding connections between things which seem totally unrelated.

GLOSSARY   **guys** tensioning ropes
              capriciousness unpredictability

THEMES, LANGUAGE & STYLE

Frost is content to present the 'fact', whether it be cleaning out a spring or mowing, and set it against 'mystery' that surrounds it. Quiet contemplation of what we do and where we are brings with it a heightened awareness of living, which may or may not lead us to moral conclusions.

Superficially Frost appears to occupy very similar ground to Wordsworth. Our relationship with nature, the simplicity of country tasks and childhood experience figure in both poets' work. Frost's poetry, however, is quieter and less grand than Wordsworth's and, unlike the earlier poet, he had personal experience of farm labour so that his feelings about the back-breaking work of apple-picking are more immediate than Wordsworth's exalted thoughts concerning the solitary reaper.

Frost deliberately avoids the passionate outpourings of the Romantic poets. He recognises the need to escape in one's imagination from time to time but as in 'Birches', he prefers to keep his feet on the ground.

Ultimately he draws satisfaction from recognising humanity and the natural environment for what they are. But the fact that the old man and the surrounding night are essentially separate does not diminish the magic and mystery of the circumstances.

Frost's particular strength is his style, which no less than Eliot's, if less dramatically, seems to capture a sense of thinking aloud. He creates the sense of the progress of the mind finding its way forward. The language never seems far from the natural movements of speech or thought. Sometimes, for instance, he pauses or hesitates. In 'After Apple-picking', for instance, the natural flow of sense is disrupted by the line breaks, exactly matching his tiredness:

> And I keep hearing from the cellar bin
> The rumbling sound
> Of load on load of apples coming in.

Identify the poems from which these words are taken.

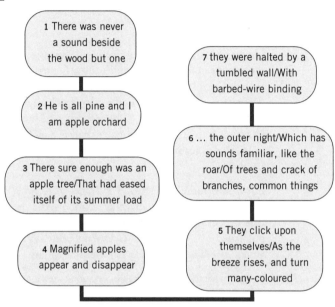

1 There was never a sound beside the wood but one

7 they were halted by a tumbled wall/With barbed-wire binding

2 He is all pine and I am apple orchard

6 ... the outer night/Which has sounds familiar, like the roar/Of trees and crack of branches, common things

3 There sure enough was an apple tree/That had eased itself of its summer load

4 Magnified apples appear and disappear

5 They click upon themselves/As the breeze rises, and turn many-coloured

Check your answers on page 96.

Consider these issues.

a Frost's feelings about the experience of physical labour.

b The ways in which Frost responds to aspects of the natural environment.

c The ways in which the poet in many of his poems seems to be talking aloud.

d How the poet maintains our interest in what seem uninteresting and undramatic subjects like mending walls or apple-picking.

R. S. THOMAS (1913–)

BACKGROUND

Ronald Stuart Thomas was born in Cardiff in 1913. He studied classics at University College, Bangor, and later trained in theology.

He was ordained as a clergyman in 1936, and, until his retirement in 1978, he was vicar in various rural parishes in mid-Wales, finally moving to the parish of Aberdaron on the Lleyn Peninsular. He learned Welsh in order to communicate fully with his parishioners, but although his early work, in particular, is deeply rooted in its Welsh location, he has only written poetry in English.

His first volume of poems, *The Stones of the Field*, was published in 1946. Other volumes followed at regular intervals. A collection of his *Selected Poems 1946–68* was published in 1973 and his *Complete Poems 1945–90* was issued in 1993 to mark his eightieth birthday.

In recent years Thomas has been associated with Welsh Nationalist politics, even expressing some sympathy with violent action.

POEMS ABOUT PEOPLE

TRAMP

For comment on this and following poems, see p. 82.

A tramp knocks at the door asking for tea. The narrator reflects on the contrast between the tramp's basic but narrow concerns and the wider social and technological horizons of the well-to-do, educated middle class. The narrator sleeps in comfort but uneasily. Is the tramp ultimately more contented?

AN OLD MAN

An old man is seen venturing out with uncertain step on an early winter's day, fearful that the wet road may be icy. The poet sees the old man embarking on the winter of his life after a harsh existence and wishes his passage through his last years to be eased, just as the sun is melting the ice that may lie in his path.

LORE

Compare the last stanza to 'Cynddylan … '

The poem celebrates life against the odds. As so many of the poems stress, life on a Welsh hill farm is unremittingly harsh, but life is for living. Job Davies is defiantly alive, whatever the elements and never-ending toil can throw at him.

SOIL

Compare with Frost's thoughts about work in 'Mowing'.

A labourer is cutting swedes, totally absorbed in his task, working into darkness. Like the tramp he does not look up; he is at one with the soil in which he seems rooted. Occasionally his knife slips so that his blood mingles with the earth from which we are fashioned.

THE HILL FARMER SPEAKS

Notice how the farmer's closeness to nature differs from that of Wordsworth, Hopkins and Frost.

In this poem the farmer's dependence on the land is depicted as so harsh and unforgiving that gentler human feelings are denied him. Despite the grinding poverty, though, he is still a man. Even so, his circumstances are so desperate, that he prefers to retreat into sharing his life with his animals, than to endure the attentions of uncomprehending outsiders.

EVANS

The poet recalls visiting a sick farmer, in his role of priest. The memory is dark and bleak. The farm and its situation is 'stark' and forbidding, but the sight of the sick man himself induces even more disturbing feelings of helplessness in the face of such desperate isolation.

CYNDDYLAN ON A TRACTOR

Think whether the poet approves or disapproves of Cynddylan.

The poet considers a circumstance which represents a break from the intimate relationship with the land that figures so strongly in his work. Cynddylan has acquired a tractor and become a 'new man'. However, as he proudly leaves the farmyard, creating comic chaos, something has changed: the farmer is now so much a part of his tractor that he has become isolated

from those activities of nature he once knew so
well.

THE POACHER

The poacher is another character who is
indistinguishable from his environment but this time he
is characterised by a whole succession of images
suggesting his invisibility and, equally importantly, how
he and nature seem to co-operate.

COMMENT   The harshness of the conditions is never far from the
forefront of these poems. The tramp sleeps rough; the
old man struggles with the icy conditions and his
uncertain future; Job Davies is defiant against the odds;
the swede gatherer is bent double in the darkness; the
hill farmer has become a recluse in order to survive;
Evans is dying in bleak isolation.

The harshness of life is mirrored in Thomas's repeated
use of vocabulary with particularly bleak associations:
'bare', 'cold', 'dark', 'gaunt', 'blood', 'rough', 'desolate',
etc.

Compare Thomas's Apart from the severity of the conditions, Thomas
depiction of the often returns to the intimacy between people and their
harshness of the environment. The swede gatherer seems almost to grow
natural out of the soil, even to the extent that his blood mixes
environment, with with it. The hill farmer is seen as almost the sum of the
the ideas suggested hostile conditions with which he must cope every day of
by Wordsworth, his life. The poacher seems to merge with landscape. In
Keats, Hopkins many ways Thomas admires this closeness to nature
and Frost. and the heroic simplicity of these people's lives. On the
other hand their lives are often narrow and insensitive.
The hill farmer has the tenacity to survive against
appalling odds but only at the price of sacrificing any
pretence of social grace. The poet wonders whether the
tramp has 'richer dreams' but Joe Davies must 'dream
small' to survive.

The picture is not all grim. Cynddylan careers out of his farmyard with careless abandon, while Job Davies has an irrepressible love of life.

POEMS ABOUT CHILDREN

FARM CHILD

The boy and the countryside that formed him are almost indistinguishable. The poem stresses how the experience of his environment has touched him in so many intimate ways to produce a natural rather than taught 'grace'.

CHILDREN'S SONG

The poem is a declaration by the children that the mysteries of their world cannot be penetrated by adults, either physically or mentally. The adult's powers of reason are of no avail in understanding the child's world nor can any amount of humouring children unlock their secrets. The poem ends by comparing the child's world to an unopened flower or an unhatched egg. The poem is an interesting variation on the theme of childhood innocence, before it is lost in adulthood.

THE EVACUEE

Look for ways the poet suggests that the girl confuses the present and her immediate past.

The wartime evacuee from the city wakes up on her first day in the country. At first there is silence – instinctively she waits for the wail of the siren – but soon the farm bursts into noisy life. She goes down to the kitchen where the farm people welcome her. Gradually, she grows in confidence and health as the memories of the 'drab town' fall away, all the time under the kind gaze of the farm hands.

COMMENT

'Farm Child' and 'Children's Song' give a new twist to an old theme, the capacity of children to live in their

own imaginative world. Unlike Wordsworth or Hopkins, Thomas does not draw any higher moral.

'Farm Child' is in some ways reminiscent of Wordsworth's 'Nutting'. Like the young Wordsworth, Thomas's child is full of the wonder of discovery but Thomas is well aware that the life of joy will all too soon be overtaken by a gruelling life on the land.

In 'Children's Song' the poet seeks to understand the world of children, but with nice irony (see Literary Terms) the poem scorns the notion that adults can ever penetrate the child's imagination.

POEMS ABOUT PLACES

ABERSOCH The poem is a personal memory of a Welsh fishing village in the sultry atmosphere of an oncoming storm. As in so many memories, only impressions remain, in this case, of the girl on the bicycle and the fishermen contentedly smoking.

THE VILLAGE

The inactivity corresponds to 'the rumours of life' in 'Abersoch'.

The village seems entirely insignificant. So little happens to break the monotony, that a dog cracking its fleas is an event. At the same time, the appearance of the girl offers an insight into the real life that lies behind the featureless surface. The village is, in fact, as important and vital to its inhabitants as any imaginary world was to the great philosopher, Plato.

COMMENT Both these village scenes are punctuated by the presence of a girl, the one on her cycle, the other moving from door to door. The girls seem to contrast with their surroundings and bring life to the scene.

SONG The song is deliberately unsentimental and unlyrical. The first stanza suggests the 'romance' of searching for the mysterious mushroom rings that appear overnight and imagines their unique delicacy. The second stanza, by contrast, describes the failure to find such a haven in the harshness of the landscape.

TWO REFLECTIVE POEMS
DAY IN AUTUMN

The poem comprises a snapshot of a moment of natural calm and repose, the memory of which will provide some mental protection against the harsh conditions that more commonly engulf the Welsh hills.

A BLACKBIRD SINGING

The poet begins by questioning why the blackbird, which should be associated with evil and dark things, in fact produces such a glorious sound. It is as though the bird's orange bill acts like the Alchemist's stone (which was reputed to turn base metal into gold) and transformed the 'notes' ore' into golden song.

The poet confirms with the reader the pleasing effects of the blackbird's song on an April evening.

The poet believes that the blackbird has an instinctive awareness of all the emotions that his ancestors have experienced but these memories always move us afresh.

COMMENT 'A Day in Autumn' expresses simple pleasure at a gentle garden scene but in 'A Blackbird Singing', the poet finds particular meaning in a similar scene.

Thomas thinks the blackbird remembers all that its ancestors have learned. The idea seems similar to that expressed by Keats in 'Ode to a Nightingale' but

Thomas is, in fact, thinking of modern theories of heredity and evolution.

The blackbird inherits a collective memory but has its own fresh voice and so it is a symbol (see Literary Terms) of the importance of tradition for a community and for the individual, together with the constant need for renewal through originality.

This is the most complex poem in the selection and may be seen as a comment on the community, Thomas's own creativity and the subtlety of creation.

THEMES, LANGUAGE & STYLE

A sense of anger at the repression of the Welsh people, which has denied them their roots, and the harshness and bleakness of their lives is the driving force of the main body of Thomas's work. Not that he is uncritical, for along with the indignation is an unsentimental awareness of the peasant's mean-spirited obstinacy.

As a priest, he was intimately involved in the world of his parishioners, but in his poetry he becomes an observer and commentator, projecting what he sees in images of sometimes fierce austerity.

The poems in this selection may be seen as a series of snapshots of the Welsh landscape and its people. Each poem presents images of Wales in close focus and forms a reflection on a particular person or scene. Some of the individual poems seem quite slight but there is a powerful thread of conviction running through them.

There is none of the elaborate richness found in Romantic poetry.

The bleakness of life in Wales is in many ways reflected in Thomas's use of a direct, plain style. For example, 'The Hill Farmer Speaks' opens with a succession of plain items of information: 'I am the farmer, – stripped of love – and thought – and grace – by the land's hardness'. Thomas builds up such details to give an image of the situation, but remains coolly analytic.

A *Identify the poems from which these quotations are taken.*

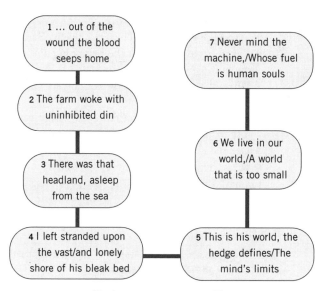

1 ... out of the wound the blood seeps home

2 The farm woke with uninhibited din

3 There was that headland, asleep from the sea

4 I left stranded upon the vast/and lonely shore of his bleak bed

7 Never mind the machine,/Whose fuel is human souls

6 We live in our world,/A world that is too small

5 This is his world, the hedge defines/The mind's limits

Check your answers on page 96.

B *Consider these issues.*

a How Thomas responds to the way people live.

b The various ways in which people may be said to be 'close to the soil'.

c Thomas's attitudes to youth and age.

d The way in which Thomas uses small details to suggest character, atmosphere (see Literary Terms) and mood.

e How, taken together, the poems build up a picture of life in Wales.

PART FOUR

STUDY SKILLS

HOW TO USE QUOTATIONS

One of the secrets of success in writing essays is the way you use quotations. There are five basic principles:

- Put inverted commas at the beginning and end of the quotation
- Write the quotation exactly as it appears in the original
- Do not use a quotation that repeats what you have just written
- Use the quotation so that it fits into your sentence
- Keep the quotation as short as possible

Quotations should be used to develop the line of thought in your essays.

Your comment should not duplicate what is in your quotation. For example:

Keats opens his poem by describing the owl being cold: 'The owl, for all his feathers, was a-cold'.

Far more effective is to write:

Keats describes the bitter, wintry conditions outside: 'The owl, for all his feathers, was a-cold'.

Always lay out the lines as they appear in the text, e.g.:

... Ah, bitter chill it was!
The owl, for all his feathers, was a-cold',

or:

'... Ah, bitter chill it was!/The owl, for all its feathers, was a-cold'.

However, the most sophisticated way of using the writer's words is to embed them into your sentence:

In order to emphasise the 'bitter chill', Keats describes the owl 'with all his feathers' as still being 'a-cold'.

When you use quotations in this way, you are demonstrating the ability to use text as evidence to support your ideas - not simply including words from the original to prove you have read it.

Everyone writes differently. Work through the suggestions given here and adapt the advice to suit your own style and interests. This will improve your essay-writing skills and allow your personal voice to emerge.

The following points indicate in ascending order the skills of essay writing:

- Picking out one or two facts about the story and adding the odd detail
- Writing about the text by retelling the story
- Retelling the story and adding a quotation here and there
- Organising an answer which explains what is happening in the text and giving quotations to support what you write

....

- Writing in such a way as to show that you have thought about the intentions of the writer of the text and that you understand the techniques used
- Writing at some length, giving your viewpoint on the text and commenting by picking out details to support your views
- Looking at the text as a work of art, demonstrating clear critical judgement and explaining to the reader of your essay how the enjoyment of the text is assisted by literary devices, linguistic effects and psychological insights; showing how the text relates to the time when it was written

The dotted line above represents the division between lower- and higher-level grades. Higher-level performance begins when you start to consider your response as a reader of the text. The highest level is reached when you offer an enthusiastic personal response and show how this piece of literature is a product of its time.

Coursework essay

Set aside an hour or so at the start of your work to plan what you have to do.

- List all the points you feel are needed to cover the task. Collect page references of information and quotations that will support what you have to say. A helpful tool is the highlighter pen: this saves painstaking copying and enables you to target precisely what you want to use.
- Focus on what you consider to be the main points of the essay. Try to sum up your argument in a single sentence, which could be the closing sentence of your essay. Depending on the essay title, it could be a statement about a character: 'Job Davies is one of the few amusing characters in Thomas's world as he never allows anything to depress him'; an opinion about a setting: 'Abersoch' and 'The Village' seem to embody the isolation and monotony of life in Wales'; or a judgement on a theme: 'I think one of Thomas's main themes is the embittering effect of harsh and gruelling conditions on people's lives'.
- Make a short essay plan. Use the first paragraph to introduce the argument you wish to make. In the following paragraphs develop this argument with details, examples and other possible points of view. Sum up your argument in the last paragraph. Check you have answered the question.
- Write the essay, remembering all the time the central point you are making.
- On completion, go back over what you have written to eliminate careless errors and improve expression. Read it aloud to yourself, or, if you are feeling more confident, to a relative or friend.

Examination essay

The essay written in an examination often carries more marks than the coursework essay even though it is written under considerable time pressure.

In the revision period build up notes on various aspects

of the text you are using. Fortunately, in acquiring this set of York Notes on *A Choice of Poets*, you have made a prudent beginning! York Notes are set out to give you vital information and help you to construct your personal overview of the text.

Make notes with appropriate quotations about the key issues of the set text. Go into the examination knowing your text and having a clear set of opinions about it.

In most English Literature examinations you can take in copies of your set books. This in an enormous advantage although it may lull you into a false sense of security. Beware! There is simply not enough time in an examination to read the book from scratch.

In the examination

- Read the question paper carefully and remind yourself what you have to do.
- Look at the questions on your set texts to select the one that most interests you and mentally work out the points you wish to stress.
- Remind yourself of the time available and how you are going to use it.
- Briefly map out a short plan in note form that will keep your writing on track and illustrate the key argument you want to make.
- Then set about writing it.
- When you have finished, check through to eliminate errors.

To summarise, these are the keys to success

- **Know the text**
- **Have a clear understanding of and opinions on the setting, themes, writer's concerns and style**
- **Select the right material**
- **Plan and write a clear response, continually bearing the question in mind**

'Wordsworth is a poet of the countryside whereas Eliot is essentially a town poet.' Discuss.

Use your first sentence or so to outline your theme.

Part 1

Wordsworth brought up in the country – several poems, especially the extracts from *The Prelude*, show how the natural landscape and country activities influenced him as he was growing up. Refer to 'Skating' and 'Elfin pinnace' episodes. Show how they contain both description of the landscape *and* its effect on his character and feelings. Make brief reference also to 'Nutting'. Include suitable quotation to support comment, e.g. reference to 'mutilated' landscape and 'sense of pain'. Contrast with more harmonious relationship in 'Skating' for example. Link also with 'Solitary Reaper'. Make further point about link between people and environment in this and 'Lucy' poems. 'To a Skylark' also combines evocation of a real bird with a moral observation.

Part 2

Refer briefly to 'Westminster Bridge' to point out that Wordsworth can also express delight in town landscape. Conclude with argument that Wordsworth found his inspiration in the countryside but his poetry involves more than simple description.

Part 3

Eliot certainly evokes scenes of town life. Even a comic poem like 'Macavity' is set in an urban environment. Refer to 'Preludes', 'Morning at the Window'. Pick out details which show depressing nature of urban environment but also show that like Wordsworth he is also concerned with its effect on people. Refer also to nature of crowds of city dwellers in 'Triumphal March'. Note that Eliot is a more detached observer than Wordsworth. Although a narrative poem like 'Journey of the Magi' included details of the countryside through which they passed, the effect is to underline the